The Mysteries of
Life, Love, and Happiness

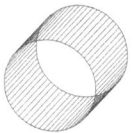

Author's Books
(As at 2016)

Non fiction

The Nature of Love and Relationships 2011, **2016** 2nd Edition
Doubts and Decisions for Living:
   Volume I: The Foundation of Human Thoughts **2014**
   Volume II: The Sanctity of Human Spirit **2014**
   Volume III: The Structure of Human Life **2014**
Relationship Facts, Trends, and Choices **2016**
The Mysteries of Life, Love, and Happiness **2016**
Marriage and Divorce Hardships **2016**
Gender Qualities, Quirks, and Quarrels **2016**
Relationship Needs, Framework, and Models **2016**

Fiction

Persian Moons 2007, **2016** 2nd Edition
Midnight Gate-opener 2011, **2016** 2nd Edition
My Lousy Life Stories **2014**

Love and Relationships Series
Eternal Loneliness

The
Mysteries
of Life,
Love, and
Happiness

Tom Omidi, Ph.D.

Copyright © 2016 by Tom Omidi
Love and Relationships Series # 2

All rights reserved. No part of this book may be reproduced, translated, or transmitted in any form or by any means—graphic, electronic or mechanical, including photocopying, recording, taping or information storage or retrieval systems—without the prior written permission of the publisher or the author.

Library and Archives Canada Cataloguing in Publication

Omidi, Tom, 1945-
Mysteries of life, love & happiness : eternal loneliness / Tom Omidi.

(Love and relationships series ; 2)
ISBN 978-0-9938006-6-5 (paperback)

1. Self-actualization (Psychology). I. Title.

BF637.S4O486 2016   158.1   C2016-902405-9

Published by Eros Books,
Vancouver, British Columbia
Canada

contact@erosbooks.net

Printed in the United States

Contents

Page

Introduction 1

PART I: Life

Chapter 1 Fundamental Thoughts about Life 7
   Humans' Fundamental Thoughts 10
   1. Reasons for Living 12
   2. Finding a Happy Life 14
   3. Making Our Lives Complete 16
   4. Enjoying Life at Its Fullest 19
Chapter 2 The Structure of Human Life 25
   Life's Main Decisions 28
   The Substance of Our Decisions and Actions 31
   The 'Self' and 'Life' Impasse 35
Chapter 3 Socioeconomic Limitations 37
Chapter 4 Personal Limitations 41
   1. Natural Limitations 41
   2. Personality Limitations 42
      Personality Aspects 43
   3. Self-imposed Limitations 48
   Limitations Due to Missed Potentialities 49
   Self-assessment 53
   The Final Judgment 56
Chapter 5 Life Limitations 57
   Life's Ultimate Limitation 57
   Timing Limitation 62
   The Meaning of Life 65
   The Main Philosophical Questions 66
Chapter 6 Life Sufferings 71
   Common Sources of Suffering 77

Contents (Cont.)

Page

PART II: Love

Chapter 7 The Nature of Love 81
   Love as a Reflection of Relationship Aspects 81
   The Meaning of Love 85
   People's Impressions and Expression of love 88
   The Importance of Defining Love 90
   Need for a Practical Love Perspective 94
   Confusion about the Meaning of Love 96
   The Effect of Hormones on Love and Relationships 100
Chapter 8 Misperceptions about Love 103
Chapter 9 Love and Loneliness Dilemmas 109
   Loneliness Dilemma 112
   The Role of Relationships 113
   Irrelevant Factors and Purposes of Marriage 117
   Relevant Factors and Purposes of Marriage 119
Chapter 10 The Mystery of Love 123
   The Outlook for Love 128
   The Power of MLove 130

PART III: Happiness

Chapter 11 'Self' and Happiness 135
   Description of Happiness 136
   Misperceptions about Happiness 137
   Characteristics of a 'Happiness' Experience 141
   The Happiness of 'Model' 144
   The Happiness of 'Ego' 150
   The Happiness of 'Self' 153
   Personality Aspects' Role for Happiness 157

Contents (Cont.)

	Page
Chapter 12 Personality and Depression	161
The Depression of 'Model'	162
The Depression of 'Ego'	164
The Depression of 'Self'	167
The Happiness/Depression Cycles	169
Depression and Suffering	172
Chapter 13 The Philosophy of Happiness	177
Managing Our Thoughts	181
The Formula of Happiness	183
Chapter 14 Forward Thinking Philosophy	187
Phase Three Reference	193
Phase Two Reference	197
Phase One Reference	201
EPILOGUE	205

Introduction

A friend asked me, "What is life? Because if God expects me the favour of living it, I'd like to know what's in it for me? Or else—if I cannot get even some peace of mind—why not end it right now and prevent all these unnecessary agony? What are all these pains and loneliness for then? All these hassles of going to school, working, accumulating wealth, searching for love and happiness, old age, sickness, stress, never-ending arguments and disappointments, and all the rest of them! Even worse, He gives us enough intelligence to suffer more for our failure to figure out life, too, instead of only hanging out aimlessly, like animals, day after day."

When I offered some of the fringe benefits of life, such as sex, pleasures, food, self-fulfilment, etc., my friend was unimpressed. He insisted that all those supposedly incentives could never make up for the suffering caused by humans' cruelty and our eternal loneliness in life. I asked him why he complained to God anyway? Is there really a God to blame for all these hassles of living? Did he believe He has intended to give humans a meaningful and pleasant life? Do not we create our gods as another attempt for defining life, to save our soul at least and perhaps hope for a happier afterlife too? Is God only another excuse for seeking relief in mysticism instead of facing reality? Is our creation of gods merely for nagging when our idiotic fantasies do not come true?

My friend said that he had to go meet someone and did not have time to answer my silly questions. His rudeness did not bother me. I know about my bad habits, including my knack for controversy.

We all have disturbing thoughts like the ones my friend was grappling with while nagging about God and life. On top of all these already confusing thoughts, we bring ourselves even more agony and loneliness with our idiotic, obsessive, endless search for love and happiness. That is the big irony! We just seem incapable of facing the reality and admitting that human logic can never find any purpose for life, even if one really existed. Our logic fails to see the simple fact that all our erratic thoughts about life and all the explorations by our smart ancestors have lead to nothing. Are not we missing something fundamental here when we keep doing the same stuff and pursue the same thoughts and goals? Have we commoners figured out anything about life after many millenniums of thinking, experimenting, philosophizing, fighting and killing, and all the other silly stuff we have done to ourselves supposedly for finding a simple way to live and being content?

Besides, I told my friend, we deserve what we get in life, because of our crooked nature, which is rotting faster every year. As society has gotten more complex, we have become sicker, our nature has deteriorated, and life has felt more unbearable to us all, too. We get fed up with our lives, and life in general, and then we take it on other individuals and our gods. Thus, we make one another and the whole society miserable too. Especially in relationships, couples blame each other for their empty lives. In effect, they blame each other for life's lack of purpose. They blame each other for their own lack of understanding about life's limited capacity to offer happiness to anybody. We are probably making God quite unhappy, too!

Unfortunately, we refuse to grasp life's sad realities and grow a more practical mentality accordingly. Despite our recurring disappointments and sufferings, we do not realize the pressure we are putting on one another with our naive views about life, mostly about an elusive happiness. We do not feel or admit that only by helping one another less selfishly, we might bear life's hardships together a bit easier. No one can elude, or do anything about, life's severe limitations in our wicked society, but only grasp and accept them with grace. Accordingly, it seems too idiotic and pathetic when we blame others, e.g., our spouses, for our stress and life's emptiness. We are too naïve and stubborn to acknowledge even these basic principles of social coexistence, yet try to discover the elaborate mysteries of life, love, and happiness. That is why our social structure and values are all falling apart too. Even worse, that is also why I felt obliged to write this book!

PART I

Life

CHAPTER ONE
Fundamental Thoughts about Life

We grow up in modern societies with the belief that the purpose of life is to find love and happiness, which are supposedly not only easy to capture as tangible attributes, but also capable of making our lives meaningful and complete. Yet, in reality, grasping even a relative sense of love and happiness, or a reliable meaning for life, proves too hard and illusive. Even worse, with such naive beliefs burdening our spirits, we cannot bring at least some level of tranquility into our lives to simulate happiness. Instead, we make living tougher for one another every day by our raw jargons and expectations about life, all in hopes of capturing some fanciful senses of love and happiness.

Throughout the history of humanity, life, love, and happiness have been alluring topics for contemplation, but proven to be only mythical concepts. After all this time and strenuous efforts to build some useful philosophies about these three supposedly fundamentals of existence, we seem totally lost all around. Yet, we seem incapable of taming our thoughts and stopping our search for a more meaningful life filled with love and happiness.

Unfortunately, life has no purpose and meaning when you get down right to it. We can fancy some ideals to humour ourselves. We can imagine and invent different means of keeping ourselves amused, usually with working harder every day, and calling our efforts 'life.' However, we must eventually get more realistic and think of life as a purposeless and meaningless existence for humans exactly as we do so readily for all other animals. It does not matter how much we wish to fool ourselves with our activities and consider our missions and passions sacred—as unique humanly virtues perhaps—, the bottom line is that we are helpless creatures born to bear the hardships of existence the same way other animals do, actually more, due to our raw intelligence and idealism. The evidence is right in front of our eyes, if we care to think a bit outside our narrow perceptions of life. It is hard to deny that the big majority of people on our planet are enduring life's hardships in different ways. Only we luckier souls must learn to view those physical and mental tortures as the basic attributes of life! Instead, we just keep worrying about the degree of happiness we must muster to capture the full purpose of life.

Nevertheless, even for us supposedly happier people in modern societies, we are only living merely on the power of our hopes day to day, imagining a kind of life that would eventually make sense to us. We also hope to grasp happiness through more pleasures and extravagance. We keep living in our fantasy worlds while calling our endless dreams and hopefulness 'life.' We prefer to stay positive and portray ourselves as a phony symbol of success and optimism, which is fine. However, reality is darker than we wish to admit and we are in fact responsible for making it so gloomy for ourselves. The sooner we accept the true reality of life and our role in causing this chaos, the sooner we can come to terms with it and stop hurting one another. Then, we can try to find our own niche in life to suffer less in the midst of this confusing social environment. We could at least be honest with ourselves privately, and try to understand life, love, and happiness in a more intelligent manner as well. We could at least try to understand what the ninety percent of people living in misery all over the world think about the meaning of life! We could have a happier life like other animals, too, if we learn to bypass the vanities propagated in society and instead grow our own sacred values.

The issues and concepts discussed in this book circle in our heads intuitively as we try to learn about our existence, find some truth about the world and people, and perhaps lead a reasonably purposeful life. We might ponder some fundamental thoughts more consciously and actively when some nagging questions about our existence and plans hit us occasionally. Nonetheless, similar thoughts run in our subconscious regularly when life dilemmas challenge us. Unfortunately, many trivial thoughts also distract our minds quite often. They cause stress and limit our chance to ponder the more fundamental thoughts, although our curiosity about existence and happiness cannot be avoided. In fact, we do not get enough chance for developing our fundamental thoughts because our brains are almost totally preoccupied with trivia. Our needs and sufferings cause an enormous amount of mundane thoughts too.

Some people may eventually find the wisdom and willpower to curb their erratic desires and thoughts in order to think deeper and feel freer. They try to maintain their integrity and sanity by defining life more realistically. However, the rest of us struggle with our unrelenting, torturous whims and thoughts all our lives, unable to decide on a meaning for life. We suffer from depression and must consume a large amount of antidepressants to go through another day. Some resort to all kinds of crimes and self-deceit to elude reality inside their shallow identities. Ironically, our deep urges and sufferings regularly trigger many spirited thoughts in our heads about 'life,' anyway. We cannot avoid our inherent curiosity about life, which are regularly raised by some fundamental thoughts. We lose our sleep and peace when our thoughts demand real justifications for our artificial needs as well as our ego-ridden ambitions and lifestyles.

Nevertheless, we know intuitively about our need for some *fundamental* thoughts to define life, grow our convictions, and develop some kind of a personal life philosophy. Only then, we believe, we can justify our existence as an intelligent person somewhat. At the very least, we like to feel some basic senses of compassion and love and a bit of peace.

Humans' Fundamental Thoughts

We are made of similar cells and DNA, but our thoughts and feelings make us who we are—so unique. Scientists believe that we make 40,000 decisions every day, which in return shows the enormity of thoughts and feelings that support or stir all those decisions day after day. Accordingly, even our simple thoughts and feelings constantly interact and clash deeply and thus expand into an enormous (and often unmanageable and stressful) pool of thoughts, emotions, and decisions at every moment.

Our thoughts can be divided into three categories. First, *fundamental* thoughts about our existence, ideals, philosophy of life, etc. They help our self-awareness, spirituality, and growth. Second, *tactical* thoughts that relate to our general learning requirements, performing our jobs, making financial plans, finding our companions, etc. These kinds of thoughts usually cause the highest level of stress and disappointment. Third, *mechanical* thoughts about our mundane affairs such as where to go, what to eat, what to buy, and similar simple thoughts that lead to the majority of our daily decisions.

Our *tactical* thoughts and decisions build (and support) the structure of our lives, e.g., schooling, working, marrying, etc. The quality of these thoughts and decisions, however, depends highly on the strength of our *fundamental* thoughts. Therefore, we should explore and analyse our fundamental thoughts in terms of their role for our growth and health, and for making wiser tactical decisions.

Normally, we do not remember even a few dozens of our thoughts in a day, if that. Yet, certain fundamental thoughts subliminally occupy the minds of intelligent humans almost constantly throughout their lives, every single day. They delineate some aspect of our lives, but also make us feel good or depressed about our surroundings and ourselves. Therefore, studying our fundamental thoughts is necessary for understanding the meaning of life and making sense of our actions and decisions. More importantly, however, we must somehow come to terms with these deep-rooted thoughts that boggle every intelligent person's mind, because that is the only way to grasp life, justify our existence, and feel good about ourselves. In fact, building a personal life philosophy by gauging our fundamental thoughts is a sacred mission we must undertake honestly and earnestly. Some of these existential thoughts are listed below.

Humans' Fundamental Thoughts

1. Our reasons for living.
2. How to build a happy life.
3. How to define a complete life in which things have value and purpose.
4. The best way to enjoy life at its fullest.
5. What is the inner 'self' and how we can use it.
6. What is the essence of humanness and whether it can be enhanced.
7. How to effect change and improve social order.
8. What a wisdom path is and how to track it.
9. What freedom is and whether it is an achievable goal.
10. How to live practically but not submissively.
11. How to nurture our positive doubts while defeating the perils of indecisiveness.
12. How to fight depression but not fear it.
13. How to make major life decisions and survive.
14. How to find a reliable companion.
15. How to optimize our physical and mental health.

The above list covers humans' main life dilemmas among many others. These integrated thoughts, and our efforts to resolve them, preoccupy any intelligent person's mind for establishing his/her general life philosophy. In fact, none of the above dilemmas (thoughts) can be truly analysed and resolved without pondering and choosing a ground for the others. Accordingly, our thoughts become too complex, fuzzy, and confusing most often—because we must find a comprehensive answer for all these life dilemmas collectively, as an exercise in self-awareness, for making our existence more authentic and meaningful. In the end, of course, 'finding the means of a happy and purposeful life' is the ultimate objective of all the fundamental thoughts on the list. All these thoughts and dilemmas are instinctive urges for finding happiness—which is a myth by the way, anyway, as will be discussed later.

Only the first four of the above noted life dilemmas are briefly reviewed in this book. However, for building a personal life philosophy, all the 15 fundamental thoughts should be studied together, as explained in this author's book, *Doubts and Decisions, Volume I*. Everybody can benefit from a well-defined personal life philosophy eventually to address all these dilemmas collectively and arrive at a comprehensive guideline for making the best use of his/her life and thoughts.

1. Reasons for Living

As we reach some level of maturity, maybe even in childhood for some geniuses, we begin to wonder about our existence. We soon want to justify it, too, as though we did not deserve to live without establishing a rationale for it. Our doubts about the purpose of our existence, along with other fundamental thoughts listed above, always roll in everybody's subconscious or unconscious minds, although most of us with lower mental activity or curiosity do not ponder them actively. Looking for a reason to live, especially, feels like an instinctual (and perhaps spiritual) urge ingrained in our genes. We cannot avoid it, and some people may commit suicide if they are oversensitive or tired of seeking that elusive justification to live. The more intelligent a person, the more s/he feels compelled to justify his/her existence, which delineates the high price we must pay for being an intelligent species. Unfortunately, it is getting harder every year to find good reasons for living within the chaotic environment and lifestyles we have created for ourselves. It is becoming more difficult to promise a bright future to our children when socioeconomic conditions are fundamentally threatened and family problems are getting out of hand. Fortunately, however, the majority of us do not give up easily, as we pursue some passive crusades to find legitimate reasons for our existence. All along, we dwell on all kinds of doubts and adopt lousy motives to continue living without ever feeling quite satisfied with our reasons. Mainly our hopes and optimism make us believe that we would eventually find a better rationale for living. We also invent some ideologies or objective to suffocate our nagging urge for finding the truth. Nevertheless, relying on some shaky purposes for living is still better than not inventing any reason at all. A lack of life purpose only heightens our frustration and depression. In a philosophical sense, people find fewer reasons for living every year, but fortunately some other instinctual urges, e.g., lust, still keep us hopeful and optimistic.

Of course, the other side of the coin is that any rational person needs even more reasons for not living. More people struggle nowadays with the thoughts and feelings of loneliness and desperation, which often appear like good reasons for not living. Still, most of us are stubborn and resilient enough to keep living anyway, as if programmed to tolerate suffering and rejections naturally. Even our doubt about the existence of some ultimate reasons for living is a positive urge to keep us going. Our doubts help us live longer, but also make us explore life, persevere, and wonder.

Nonetheless, our lifelong urge to justify our existence is an added pressure of living by itself while it also complicates our thoughts and feelings constantly. In fact, living is too difficult, because we feel obliged to justify both an eager existence and early exit, while no rationale seems to exist for either. Oddly, not having a good reason for living or dying does not automatically justify, and lead to, the other option. This deep inner conflict creates the most fundamental doubt in our lives—the biggest dilemma we struggle with forever. That is the question Shakespeare imposed, "To be or not to be?" The conflict Hamlet faces is because he needs reasons for both, although the emphasis appears to be on finding a justification for living. Our struggle to find a valid reason for either option never ends. Period. Meanwhile, we just plough on through life, suffer, think, enjoy, until we die.

As we get older, we realize even the futility of our hopes and dreams, let alone our lasting struggles to find a reason for living. We learn to merely amuse ourselves somehow until the end arrives. We grasp the futility of all those worries, thoughts, and solemn feelings that have crippled us for no tangible outcome. We eventually admit that life has no purpose when we are old and tired, if not sooner. This is a sad conclusion that poses another fundamental question for youth—about living an inherently purposeless life, if going by the testimony of wise elderly. Well, that is why they prefer to ignore the elderly advice!

The irony is that, at the end, we face a substantially more fundamental thought as soon as we realize two basic facts that: 1) No philosophical reasons exist for living, and 2) no rational reasons exist for not living either. Back to square one! Then, our new and urgent fundamental thought (and dilemma) would be: Can we learn to build a useful life for ourselves based on the above two simple facts without letting these existential thoughts and feelings torture us? This is a major conflict and intellectual challenge for many people and it can be resolved somewhat only after we learn to build at least a personal life philosophy.

2. Finding a Happy Life

Obviously, all our thoughts and actions are for one ultimate purpose: To lead a happy, healthy life in a meaningful manner. Well, if life has no particular purpose, can we at least find a means of being happy? Our innate optimism and hope make us believe in the possibility of finding happiness and tranquility. Our pride also goads us to believe that not finding happiness is a direct reflection of our unworthiness and failure. Occasionally, we get a taste of this elusive happiness, which raises our hopes about the possibility of making it permanent. Thus, we look for the wisdom of doing so by seeking all kinds of advice from gurus and experts. Part III of this book is devoted to a detailed discussion of 'self' and happiness. It attempts to identify the characteristics of happiness, but mainly suggests that a special personality and outlook are needed to maintain happiness rather permanently. In line with building that proper (but rather unconventional) personality, our ultimate happiness depends on how well we come to terms with all the fundamental thoughts listed at the beginning of this chapter. We need the right personality and convictions to resolve these dilemmas and a variety of doubts, feelings, and thoughts that overwhelm us.

An authentic 'personal life philosophy' must also augment a 'proper personality' to manage our doubts and decisions in life, balance the cycles of happiness and depression, and find tranquility. This combination would help us choose the right values and a simple lifestyle, and develop the right mindset and priorities. A proper personality nurtures a solid personal philosophy intuitively or through self-awareness. Accordingly, the person learns to adhere to his/her convictions and beliefs regardless of all the external forces that try to influence his/her thoughts and feelings.

A main challenge in life, of course, is to understand the characteristics of a proper personality and build authentic personal convictions in our materialistic societies. Even more difficult, however, is to admit the necessity of developing our beliefs and convictions. Unless a person is somehow blessed with at least some inherent goodness and curiosity for gauging his/her life options, s/he hardly sees the need for a personal overhaul or life philosophy. Thus, the question is, 'How a person with no inherent goodness or wisdom would ever care to consider his/her life options objectively and strive to build a personal life philosophy?' What other incentives may motivate him/her to change his/her lifestyle, and find happiness? How people with formed personalities and crooked philosophies can find happiness without first reassessing themselves and their ideologies? How can we find happiness before making a major overhaul in our mentality? How can we free ourselves from the luring rewards of materialism to build self-reliance and some sense of spirituality?

Answering these questions is difficult, but some guidelines to achieve this horrendous task are suggested throughout this book. Three points are clear though: (1) Finding happiness requires a proper mindset and personality, (2) pursuing an authentic life philosophy for finding happiness gradually leads to development of an ideal personality, and conversely, (3) an ideal personality would have no difficulty in choosing a personal philosophy that leads to some notion of happiness.

3. Making Our Lives Complete

We often feel a sense of emptiness and doubt the quality of our lives. Of course, external factors and luck always affect our moods, but mostly our boredom causes self-doubts and depression. Our dreams about a 'complete' life feel either unachievable or meaningless again after a while. Usually, we imagine a complete life in sitting at the beach with a cold drink, a handsome companion keeping us amused, and lots of money to buy whatever we wish. Alas, not even all these rewards can give us a complete life.

If we get a little more philosophical, we helplessly question the value of our routine activities and resent wasting our precious lives so mindlessly. We like to know what else is out there that could make our lives a little more meaningful, and possibly complete. We blame ourselves for the void and not finding a more sensible path. During our struggles for a meagre subsistence, or while accumulating enormous wealth, after doing the same things over and over again, with every failure or accomplishment, we still doubt the purpose of spending our lives on those routines and dread the lingering shallowness of our existence. All along, in fact, we also feel the inherent vanity of life altogether.

We usually force ourselves out of these depressing moods by engaging even deeper in our routine lives and struggles, or seek more pleasures. These are the best remedies and defence mechanisms we have been able to fathom. Yet, a subtle sense of incompleteness resides in our subconscious throughout our lives and makes all our goals and struggles feel like a bottomless abyss. One day, this feeling becomes too deep and fundamental no matter how often and hard we fight the moods of 'incompleteness.' Therefore, one purpose of our personal life philosophy is to find a simple definition of life, instead of worrying about its completeness and means of enhancing the quality of our superficial lives. The prevalent lifestyles can never offer a complete life, nor can give our existence an essence.

The feeling of emptiness often surges from boredom, but not necessarily from the lack of activities and excitement. We may attempt to relieve our tensions by getting involved with more activities, pampering our sexuality, taking on new challenges, travelling all over the world, and looking for exciting ventures. However, these distractions would not resolve our sense of void and vanity in the long run. Only when our adventures and experiences find authentic values or offer a new learning dimension, we grasp that mystical sense of spiritual completeness. Other activities only add to our feelings of boredom and void, despite their potential for inducing temporary relief. We usually try to keep busy somehow or socialize non-stop to suffocate the lingering feeling of emptiness, which is often on top of our normal sense of loneliness, even when we are in a relationship. For spiritual completeness, as an alternative way of living, we must prepare for a long inner journey to overhaul our mentality, however.

Contrary to common perception, a complete life is not structured around 'things.' Rather, it depends on how effectively we use those special life 'resources' we inherently own, such as our potentialities, passion, compassion, and spirituality. Struggling for more of everything simply wastes our most precious resources of life, i.e., time, energy, and intelligence. However, people normally perceive 'completeness' in owning more of every *thing* that is out there. The mentality of our modern societies revolves around greed and egotism instead of needlessness and selflessness. We enjoy wasting everything, both material and mental, with our addiction to consumerism.

Our struggle to get more of everything we already have only raises the bar endlessly toward that imaginary completeness. Aiming for a balance of things, not more of everything, and an effective use of life resources are naturally the secrets of a complete life. The less time, money, and mental energy is spent on things, the more resources can be devoted to fundamental thoughts and authentic needs in life, which provide a much higher value for 'completing' our lives, in terms of both the number of years (quantity) we live and what we do (quality.) A 'complete life' requires a full range of worthy thoughts, feelings, actions, and principles (life values) to fulfil a large amount of social and personal responsibilities. During this process, we seek the means of true happiness (peace of mind), bring 'self' in control of our actions and decisions, find a path of wisdom according to our life philosophy, etc. Our limited energy and intuition should guide us explore new, soulful experiences and attain self-actualization, which is the shortest path for normal people to get a sense of completeness and divinity.

A complete life contains a variety of simple events and ventures that produce purposeful learning and growth experiences, and at the same time, create childlike excitements and sense of achievements. Contrary to the common perception, 'complete' does not imply a stationary state in which everything reaches its perfection. Rather, a complete life is always dynamic and requires a high degree of change and risks. Two levels of challenges recur in a complete life. First, the challenges and plans necessary for maintaining our basic needs and health effectively—to build up a stable state of mind and body. Second, the challenges and plans that goads the process of personal growth—the dynamism of a complete life. This growth is achieved by new learning experiences and purposeful efforts throughout our normal lives. Growth is a natural process that contains schooling, learning, working, building a path of wisdom, making a family and raising children perhaps, plus all other routine decisions, actions, struggles, pleasures, and doubts. We must push and measure this natural growth for defining our existence and building our life philosophy. All these small experiences also provide the texture and beauty that add to the 'completeness' of our lives.

We can strive forever to explain some aspects of a complete life and choose certain fundamentals to achieve it. However, beyond all these experimentations, we can conclude that life by itself has no special properties to make it complete. We may assume that our universe is perfect as it is, but even that would be only another subjective judgment. The perfection or completeness of life is created in the mind of each person based on the soundness of his/her life philosophy and personal experiences. Therefore, in a philosophical sense, 'A complete life is the one that we know how to create for ourselves.'

4. Enjoying Life at its Fullest

To most of us, enjoying life means having as much pleasure and extravagance as we can possibly muster. We rely mostly on our drives for sexuality, love, possession, and power to maximize our chances for enjoying life. For achieving these appealing goals, we adopt superficial values, waste time and energy to build a phony personality, and maintain a busy but boring lifestyle. This demented mentality has grown fast in modern societies and still people wonder why they are not enjoying their lives as much as they think they should or deserve. All those seeming pleasures actually make them feel lonelier and emptier every day. Despite our strenuous struggles to enjoy life and find the means of happiness, we still feel the incompleteness and emptiness of our lives. The rising rate of social stress and family breakdowns are the main symptoms of our present shoddy mentality. No matter how much pleasure, possessions, and power we enjoy, at the end we still face the same dilemma: How to make our lives a bit more peaceful or somewhat meaningful.

Therefore, it seems that maximizing our life enjoyment is merely a matter of reaching certain level of maturity and contentment. This happens only when we grow a mentality to perceive our life *complete* (meaningful and enriching) as is for a selfless, self-fulfilling person. 'Enjoying life in its fullest' and 'making our lives complete' are the two sides of the same coin. Thus, for enjoying life we must again emphasize on making our lives meaningful and complete. But how must we go about doing this?

Ironically, we must first accept that no inherent 'complete' life exists to maximize our life enjoyments. Only we, personally, can define and make our lives relatively enjoyable and meaningful by adopting a simple life philosophy. In return, our simple life philosophy must contain all these basic principles about humans' natural needs. Ultimately, the 'completeness' of life comes from inside us in the form of mental energy to use our unique potentialities and opportunities for reaching contentment and self-reliance. We cannot define one unique purpose, e.g., happiness, for life. We cannot devise a formula of completeness based on a combination of certain life purposes either. In fact, the irony is that the simpler the lifestyle we adopt, the more complete and enjoyable life becomes. If these conclusions are valid, they reflect why life cannot be complete (or meaningful) in itself beyond our personal mentality and inner strength.

Yet, we exhaust ourselves with our idle attempts to find the meaning of life, make it complete, and enjoy it as much as possible. Accordingly, we follow a lifestyle that feels incomplete and causes only more depression. A sign of incomplete life is the amount and intensity of our never-ending regrets for the opportunities lost and decisions not made, or made hastily or foolishly. Regrets could also be a sign of wisdom. However, if we cannot reverse or ignore the repercussions of our earlier mistakes, we can hardly hope for a meaningful and peaceful life. We can always try to make the best of our existing circumstances, but for reaching a permanent inner peace, we must make certain efforts and decisions at the right time. To have a complete life, we must plan for it—mostly in terms of life philosophy and path. We cannot 'live in the now' and expect to have a complete life too. Rather, planning is crucial for minimizing the unnecessary struggles of life and for avoiding irreversible mistakes that could cause lasting grief and regrets. Planning is for making our critical life decisions in a timely manner, while we also depend on our instincts and doubts to help us with those decisions. Foresight and planning are mostly for not getting trapped in inescapable and regretful situations.

Another big irony is that, while life has no real purpose, we must set many personal purposes for our lives and thus make it 'meaningful' *merely* for our needs according to our objective mind and for helping us maintain our health. *The completeness of our lives depends on how consciously we try to define one for ourselves according to proper values.* The ideas offered throughout this book can help on this regard, especially about the fact that life's 'completeness' depends on our ability to use our potentialities and time wisely. A big emphasis must be placed on one's timing and diligence regarding major life decisions, which have the highest *potential* for contributing to the completeness of one's life.

Every day, we hear million simple examples of how we, as parents, and society in general, brainwash and spoil our children. We push them develop their crooked value systems and fanciful ambitions, which have no meaningful purpose and instead mislead them altogether when the time comes for making their major life decisions. Accordingly, we abolish their chances to be good parents or spouses in their own relationships.

One traditional principle always makes sense: There is a 'right time' for every decision and every doubt. We can leisurely follow our dreams and enjoy righteous experiences throughout our lives, achieve our goals, love, etc. However, there is a 'right time' in our lives for certain things. There are only certain years that we can enjoy childish thoughts and plays. There are right times for building a career and a family. There is a right time for making a decision about marrying a particular person. There is a right time for understanding the strengths of our marriages and preventing their demise. There are *right times* for making all critical decisions of life. If we stand by and let the opportunity slip away, or make hasty decisions, we face many disappointments in life. There is also an 'optimal time' for less critical life decisions, which are still important, e.g., for completing a college education if one intends to have one.

It seems hard for most of us to accept that only simpler life purposes fulfil the inner needs of 'self' and provide experiences beyond egotistical or materialistic values. Every piece of music can be rediscovered over and over. Every plant and flower has a different property, delicacy, or fragrance that we can feel for the first time. Our thoughts can stir the boundless energy that leads to unique creations and valuable experiences of tranquility. We can enjoy the feeling of achievement by doing small things like gardening, writing a short story, painting, meditation, or physical exercise.

Enjoying life is obviously more than having an occasional feeling of ecstasy, or even getting the sense of 'completeness' resulting from personal achievement and self-actualizing experiences. To enjoy life, the cycles of happiness experiences must be continuous and self-feeding, while we manage the pressures of depression cycles effectively too. We do not necessarily need major achievements and self-actualizing experiences to attain the highest sense of completeness and joy. Rather, we need many simple experiences that are complementary in the way various potentialities of a person are challenged and utilized. We need 'self' driven experiences, since only they release the huge amount of energy and joy that flow naturally within us. We need more of the experiences that are not based on winning and hostility, but rather on giving and forgiving. We do not need more pleasures and sexuality to enjoy life at its fullest, but only some compassion.

CHAPTER TWO
The Structure of Human Life

We have different lives and destinies. Yet, in the larger scope of the universe and social order, we all travel the same road and reach the same destination. Like other species, we have a life expectancy, a range of strengths and weaknesses, special habits and defence mechanisms, certain habitats and existential characteristics, etc. Our relatively higher intelligence goads our drive for individualism and a variety of goals and lifestyles. Yet, a natural process defines the boundaries of our existence, while we proceed within certain social parameters, mostly driven by our genetic inheritance and social norms. After all, we are still only one infinitesimal part of the whole existence, in spite of our amazing initiatives, all the skyscrapers we can build, and the technologies we have mastered. Both the natural laws (our instincts) and social order drive us to follow a rather uniform path of life hypnotically.

Thus, we all go through certain life phases and do similar things to prepare ourselves to live, multiply, raise our offspring, and die. In the process, we hope to satisfy our physical and psychological needs, both the instinctual ones and those we have developed artificially throughout the history. We have created things and thoughts that we believe are useful to us, although we can never be sure about that. We have already demonstrated how some of our demented thoughts make us capable of destroying our cultures and lives. We kill each other directly, or engage in life processes and activities that would eventually destroy our societies and human existence.

Nonetheless, all these human attributes have evolved into a peculiar life structure over several millenniums according to our perceptions of our identity and needs, and now it directs us uniformly within globally predefined parameters, although some of us are richer or happier. Within this ordained structure, everybody participates in similar processes and activities, instinctually or habitually, and pursues similar ambitions as a matter of social expectation. We entertain similar thoughts and do similar things to survive within this structure. This social structure also imposes a rather fixed mentality and a common set of goals for us to follow. It imposes major decisions and doubts on everybody to dwell upon within an inherent order during three definable life phases. However, does this life structure make real sense? We must answer this question to our 'self' and soul.

Like a tree that has roots, a trunk, branches and fruits, the structure of human life is also constructed around some foundation, purposes, activities, and outcome during three life phases. In the first phase, we prepare ourselves for the life that lies ahead of us. We spread our roots and develop our strengths and primary wisdom to get ready for the challenging and demanding phases awaiting us. In the second phase, we develop our careers and family lives, which, similar to the trunk of a tree, comprise the main body or purpose of our lives. In the final phase, we expect to reap the fruits of a lifetime of efforts and growth. This common vision and approach to life feels natural to us all, but are our thought foundation, purposes, activities, and life outcomes sensible for a thinking human or are we still living soullessly like a tree?

The definition of a structure is significant particularly for identifying the nature of the main decisions and actions needed in life. The intention is not to generalize life. Similar to a tree that has many branches and somehow signifies its uniqueness, individuals' distinctive dimensions are very interesting by themselves. They influence our progress, way of thinking, and our preferences in making decisions and taking actions. Our decisions and actions are different, because we see the same things differently, and because we judge a situation or person according to our personality and beliefs. However, despite our differences in judgment, values, decisions and actions, we all must follow the same road—a general life structure fitting our social values and culture. This life structure reflects the eventual commonality of human thoughts and actions in pursuit of their personal goals, for the purpose of survival, adaptation, and for getting other people's approval and cooperation. Our needs and struggles to adapt create a uniform structure for human life, though it has become a rather dysfunctional mechanism nowadays.

We cannot challenge this inevitable truth about humans' life and their perceptions. The only problem is that we follow this life structure rather blindly according to certain facts and myths surrounding us. We have learned certain things about life and ourselves, but the unknown reality is getting wider in scope and affecting the structure of our lives significantly too. We know that our physics (and existence) is only a by-product of an accident, when one *particular* sperm luckily finds its way to a *particular* ovary in a special moment. But our souls? We do not know where it comes from and where it returns to. As long as our physics is healthy and conscious, we have a personality and a set of characteristics that contain both our physics and soul. Some of us know better how to envision and combine these two features of humanness, whereas a great majority of us can only understand, and stagnate mostly at, the physical level.

This author's book, *Doubts and Decision for Living, Volume III,* provides a detail study of humans' life structure, its characteristics, and the way we helplessly follow its guidelines so naively. Many questions can be raised about the validity of this structure and our hypnotic attachment to it. At the end, we may still believe that it provides the best option for living despite our inability to justify its meaning and purposes. However, by learning more about this dull life structure, we might be able to perceive and change at least a few aspects of it for ourselves for getting a bit more sense out of our existence. Most people are hoping to figure out the meaning of their activities and ambitions within this frivolous life structure when they say they want to 'find the meaning of life.'

Life's Main Decisions

The essentiality of our decisions and actions are supposedly measured by the severity of their consequences, risks, or opportunities missed. Some decisions and actions can change one's life direction and they may cause lifelong agonies and depression. Some decisions and actions can result in irreversible mistakes, or losing some precious opportunities, due to erroneous or delayed choice of a life path. In all, the essentiality of life decisions and actions is gauged by the high level and longevity of their impacts on the overall welfare and happiness of a person. In particular, the outcomes of decisions regarding our careers, aspirations, and marriages could be vastly risky and consequential. Therefore, they constitute essential life decisions. Yet, customarily, we view and handle them as life's routine decisions. Thus, hardly we realize their severity, potential consequences, or our missed opportunities, all due to our Egos, procrastination habits, or miscalculations.

Naturally, essential life decisions would have been quite easy to make if we could truly feel the potential agony of negative outcomes (e.g., a bad marriage) in advance. However, since we cannot, we should develop a reliable foundation of thoughts and life philosophy for not only assessing our decisions diligently at the outset, but also fighting the vast amount of agonies and disappointments that our bad decisions cause. We can blame life and other people's wickedness, but usually our naive decisions are behind our failures. Of course, two points must be noted here as well. First, often destiny plays dirty hands in making many of our decisions go sour—as if perhaps God had a more divine plan in mind for us behind the scene. Second, it seems that some of us have a special knack for making wrong choices and decisions despite our good intentions and reasonable diligence—as if we had a pact with Satan to ruin our lives. We cannot fight these inevitable forces in life, but remembering all these points should at least give us a bit more sense of caution and self-awareness.

Unfortunately, most of us neither have developed a reliable foundation of thoughts, nor believe in other people's opinion and advice, even if they were big philosophers and scientists. We do not trust even individuals that normally care for us. In fact, we distrust almost everybody and the society rather logically due to all the wickedness out there. Worst of all, our criteria and values for decision-making are infected by crooked social norms. It is hard for us, firstly, to imagine the possibility of making better life decisions by adopting more authentic values (including ethics and morality). In fact, we have become addicted to a large variety of superficial values that our societies propagate—mainly in terms of consumerism and pomposity. Secondly, most of us are emotional, driven by our sexual urges, and live in the now too. That is, we are too dissolved in our phony worlds and personalities to appreciate the real life essentialities or the importance of certain life-changing decisions. Thirdly, it would be difficult for most of us to give up social rewards of our shallow *perceived world*, e.g., love and belongingness, in pursuit of alleged opportunities and serenity of an illusive *real world* that might eventually result from following a more authentic lifestyle.

Setting life priorities is also a matter of personal judgment. Accordingly, people interpret the essentiality of life decisions and actions differently. Individuals' outlook on life determines how significant or essential some decisions or actions seem to them. People who pursue life for pleasures only, those who seek power per se, those who emphasize on wealth, those who need constant approval and love, or stoics, they all have different life outlooks. Thus, each group has a different standard of 'essentiality' for similar decisions and actions, although they all have a somewhat similar understanding of life structure.

Based on this book's discussions, we can divide essential decisions and actions into two major types. The first category of decisions and actions relates to the requirements of living in society, maintaining our relationships, satisfying our economic needs, etc. Let us call them 'life' decisions. The second type of decisions relates to our eagerness to learn about our personal identity, spirituality, and real inner needs. Let us call them 'self' decisions. In this regard, we make decisions to adopt and pursue a specific life philosophy, build a solid foundation of thoughts, and take specific actions to maintain a high level of awareness and 'self'-control. The objective is to satisfy our self-actualization and spirituality needs by understanding more about our 'self.'

For people who do not grasp, or care to realize, the essence of 'self' and its unique needs, no decisions or actions regarding the second type seem necessary, let alone considering them 'essential.' This group, which holds a majority in society, has no patience or interest in these kinds of questions and efforts. Thus, they concentrate solely on 'life' decisions, i.e., socioeconomic matters and relationships. On the other hand, in the eyes of the minority who believes in understanding 'self' and leading a 'self'-controlled life as an essential guide and philosophy, placing emphasis merely on socioeconomic decisions and actions appears ridiculous. They believe the other group is not only missing the real meaning of life, but also causing their own agonies and pains merely out of their naivety—not to mention their high share of irresponsibility for creating the chaos in society.

For a prudent person, it is essential to at least understand the implications of, and relations between, 'life' and 'self' decisions and actions. We need this awareness for creating some form of harmony between social life and personal enlightenment. It is hard to imagine how we can go through life without some notion of 'self' included in our foundation of thoughts to support our decisions and actions. It seems that our personal problems and social pains are the outcome of our shortsightedness, and the lack of a good foundation of thoughts and 'self'-control. Nevertheless, this is the reality that many of us have chosen as our only option. Thus, we continue our lives in vain without understanding the reasons for our living and suffering.

On the other hand, only a small group can concentrate solely on 'self' questions and decisions, e.g., self-awareness and divinity. They find the strength and courage to break away from the mainstream and pursue seclusion and enlightenment as their sole path of life. This mentality and approach is not something that many of us can understand or attempt, so we do not spend much time explaining it.

For most of us, adopting a middle ground or moderation seems perhaps the most sensible approach. We just hope to combine the benefits and wisdom of both 'life' and 'self' decisions and actions to attain the highest level of personal fulfilment and peace. At least, we may be able to regain some relative freedom and curb some of our sufferings. At a middle ground, we can learn about ourselves and our life options without giving up so much of our regular life commitments and pleasures. At the same time, we can apply the wisdom we earn from 'self' decisions and actions to our social life situations directly.

The Substance of Our Decisions and Actions

A right mix of 'life' and 'self' related decisions and actions can enrich our lives and reduce our sufferings. Our occasional encounters with our spirituality urges, while pursuing our normal lives, might raise our interest for 'self' awareness and possibly making our life decisions more in line with non-materialistic values. For example, we may consider devoting a part of our lives to some humanitarian causes. Building the foundation of our thoughts and choosing a life philosophy require learning about 'self' too. These moments of awakening happen to many people. Some pause and pay attention to those profound thoughts (because they soothe their minds). They discover something new about themselves and their inner power. They may take these signs seriously as a guide for exploring the deepest aspect of their 'self.' However, most of us bypass these callings quickly and impatiently, or do not follow them up seriously. Thus, we never get the chance to at least explore the alternatives to our mundane lives. We continue to suffer when we never get a chance to discover our real essence of being and free our souls.

Realistically, we do not know how to deal with the inner voices and questions circling in our heads, especially if we do not have the time, or when the messages contradict our lifestyles and values. However, with some patience and practice, we can learn to absorb these messages and give a benefit of a doubt to the possibility of a more serene life outside the prevalent social structure.

Transcending to the real world sphere and realizing our 'self' occur gradually, of course. We must learn the basics first, and then mature by getting deeper into our unconscious mind and 'self' personality. During this slow process of transcendence to a new realm and realizations, we learn more about our inherent identity, including our weaknesses and potentialities. Only through sacrifice, reserved apprehension, and wisdom, we may climb the mountain of the truth and reach the summit. Only through patience and conviction, we can achieve selfhood and feel the results of our meditations and convictions. Nobody can jump beyond his/her *primary wisdom* (which evolves slowly) for a higher vision of life—not even with the use of drugs or artificial stimuli. Unfortunately, the majority of us fail, because we look for a quick solution and salvation, or at least a sign of wisdom, when we have not even learned how to do a basic self-analysis or create a no-thought experience for ourselves.

The secret for finding a relative peace of mind and happiness lies in our ability to develop a middle ground, in which both 'life' and 'self' choices are simultaneously and continuously interactive, and justifiable too. Both 'life' and 'self' orientation are important within the structure of human life and require our scrutiny and right decisions. As noted, however, our emphasis on 'life' decisions, has limited our ability to bring meaning and serenity to our daily routines.

Discussions in this book can reveal a long list of 'major decisions' that we face in life about:
- The purpose of life and means of happiness.
- The kind of life philosophy that fits our personality, needs, and plans.
- Our values, beliefs, and convictions.
- How to manage our thoughts and create no-thought moments.
- Our authentic (versus superficial) personal needs and how to go about satisfying (or curbing) them.
- Our long-term life objectives and a plan to work toward them.
- The risk oriented opportunities and timing of them.
- Our real potentialities and limitations.
- Monitoring our three personality aspects and finding 'self'-control.
- The career we should choose.
- Gaining our financial sense and living within our limits.
- The means and criteria to choose a spouse.
- Having children or not, how to nurture them, and what our role should be.
- Etc.

The above decisions and actions also raise many basic questions, such as the followings:
- Why do we feel, act, and choose in certain ways?
- Why do we educate ourselves or learn things?
- Why do we need friends and companionship?
- Why do we work?
- What are the sources of our fulfilments?
- What are our financial resources?
- How should we set our life priorities and expectations?

- How do we feel about our relationships with people and Nature?
- Etc.

We ponder these questions regularly, but only superficially within the context of our mundane busy lives. They appear to surge from our unconscious mind, more in a form of an inner voice (or conscience) that seeks profound, philosophical answers. In fact, these questions reflect the inherent urgency of 'life' and 'self' decisions in some combination, depending on how deeply we view them or act upon them. We cannot avoid them even if we are the most pragmatic 'life' oriented person. These questions, and our corresponding decisions and actions, inherently construct the structure of life. We face them regardless of our emphasis on certain inner needs, and whether or not we have a profound foundation of thoughts to draw upon. However, we do not pause adequately to contemplate these questions in some depth in relation to the purpose of living and for being a better person.

For those devoted to 'self' and in search of a profound foundation of thoughts, a different concern may also exist. The challenge for this group is to transform those profound thoughts into practical actions. We may have been successful in preparing a sense of 'self' commitment and some kind of foundation of thoughts to guide us through life. But then when it comes to act upon our commitments or convictions, we fall short of our objectives and standards. When the time comes for us to act with integrity, we fail to adhere to our 'self'-control rules and we get tempted by money, love, pleasures, greed, sex, and other personal weaknesses that often take over our profound commitments and character. Or sometimes, we simply become lazy in pursuing our commitments and objectives. Or we lose our patience and conviction.

For many reasons, we often fail to implement the ideals and standards we have set in our foundation of thoughts. We may then take this failure as a major flaw and a sign of irreparable personal weakness. We may even revert to a superficial or passive/aggressive personality eventually. We then give up our idealistic vision of 'self' and a commitment to delve into the depth of our being.

The 'Self' and 'Life' Impasse

Therefore, 'life' and 'self' appear like two opposing poles on the mysterious realm of human existence. The more we emphasize on 'life,' the more we lose sight of our 'self.' Conversely, attending to 'self' requires letting go of 'life' drastically, at least in the form we perceive and live it merely according to our desires and ambitions. Our struggles to find 'self' within 'life' (or 'life' within 'self') only increase our inner conflicts and we get more impatient and frustrated with people and ourselves. Both life and self feel like abstract mysteries that we can never grasp, let alone integrate. We try hard to at least find a meaning for life. Yet, it persists to remain a mystery, like a vague notion only teasing and confusing us. We feel the same way about 'self,' too, which appears to be an ambiguous concept beyond our reach. Yet, we know that both 'life' and 'self' are real, as inherent features of human existence, even though we are unable to define or find them. We suspect that 'life' would reveal its true meaning only if we find our 'self.' And we suspect that 'self' emerges only within the context of the true life, which is pure and simple, unlike the lifestyles we are pursuing nowadays. These facts suggest that 'life' and 'self' are actually complementary (instead of opposing) poles for signifying human existence. They are the prerequisites of each other and only together reveal their meanings and significance.

Fortunately, many of us believe that our curiosity and struggles to find life and self are justified. Many clues show that our seemingly vain attempts to find the essence of our existence, the 'self,' within 'life' is not an ambitious or naïve adventure, but rather an instinctual urge that might be the key to our salvation. And our seemingly futile struggle to find the essence of 'life' within 'self,' the free being, is not a passing romanticism, but rather a natural calling.

We must live with this paradox throughout our lives. Meanwhile, we hope to make the right decisions for living, too, at least for stopping our naive or egotistical choices that cause us too much suffering. It gets difficult to build a reliable life philosophy when we seem to have difficulty understanding even the meanings and contents of life and self as two main pillars and puzzles in the realm of our mysterious existence. Still, in spite of this paradoxical barrier, we must find a means of developing a solid personality and foundation of thoughts for making those major life decisions listed on page 33. In fact, the difficulty of making such vital decisions stems from our failure to figure out the meanings of life and self at some basic level at least. After all, it is not easy for most of us to create a right balance between 'life' (our worldly desires) and 'self' (our spiritual aspirations).

CHAPTER THREE
Socioeconomic Limitations

Life has become more obscure the more we have tried to build a social structure to help us. We are social creatures by reputation, but lack the minimum sense for relating effectively or being sociable without hurting one another so regularly. In fact, we have made it too difficult for ourselves to have a rather relaxed existence, let alone finding a meaning for life to support our ideals or even offer some simple norms of living. We hope to expand our capabilities and opportunities by spreading social values and systems, but in fact cause a great deal of havoc and stress for ourselves and create all sorts of socioeconomic limitations in the process.

It is sad that we are becoming more susceptible every day to erratic forces beyond our control. We are not talking about fate or natural forces in the universe, but rather the manmade social and economic systems that dictate our way of thinking and living. Our social structure has become too complex to understand and cope with. We no longer know how to live naturally while our attitude and mentality shape around many superficial social norms. Ironically, we have lost, at the same time, our faith in the systems and mechanisms that build the social structure, including our political and judicial institutes. Family values have deteriorated drastically, too, due to social and economic pressures. The nature and purpose of family relationships have changed immensely in the last few decades. Partners have extreme difficulty to relate or understand each other's expectations. Everybody dreams and demands erratically in their relationships because no moral standards exist to apply as an objective, basic guideline. We have discarded our traditional family values, but have no new guidelines to curb our wild imaginations and rising idiosyncrasies. We are living in fantasy with our naïve life outlook and relationship expectations. We adopt fake identities to adapt and prosper, thus lose a chance to explore who we really are and what the objectives of our being and socializing are. All these routine pressures impose immense limitations for building a simple life.

In particular, our children are seriously confused about social values and ways. They lack some reliable criteria to gauge and build their life structure and define their companionships, which have become quite chaotic and frustrating for them. Many of them desire to free themselves from the anxiety of living in this environment, but do not know how or often end up choosing another lousy alternative for living and thinking. All we need to do is to look around ourselves and see how senseless the crimes of the recent decades have become and how unhealthy our environment and living conditions are becoming. The other day, on Friday August 16, 2013, three teenagers in Oklahoma City gunned down and murdered an Australian student, Christopher Lane, because, as one of them said, "We were bored."

The other night, a documentary on TV highlighted the life of a bunch of university graduates turned prostitutes in order to pay back their student loans. It is hard not to wonder about the deep demise of our social structure and values. It is hard not to wonder about the youth's mentality and our teachings to them. It is hard not to doubt the value of university education when job markets cannot help university graduates. All that education does not even teach people anything about basic human integrity, self-worth, and ethics. What are all these efforts good for then?

Random shootings, families kidnapping or killing own members, teenagers becoming murderers for a few dollars or out of boredom, police shooting innocent people unnecessarily only out of arrogance, unemployment and the absence of an economic infrastructure in line with population growth, greed and disproportionate distribution of wealth, pollution and destruction of natural and economical resources, obsession with sexuality, more consumerism and capitalistic ideologies, senseless suicides, on and on and on. The list of crazy acts and values that we are supposed to understand and deal with, and the limitations that we are expected to plan our lives within are growing larger but tighter. The consequence of all these pressures is a deep state of confusion and helplessness to grasp the meaning of our lives or anything around us. Many of us have already lost self-control and attempt crazy acts, such as bombing buildings and killing hundreds of innocent people. Who can really find a meaning for his/her existence in this environment when every one of us has become a part of the problems even as we try to be a better person?

Despite our children's potentialities and efforts to achieve certain goals, the impact of external limitations, i.e., social and economic systems, is extreme and capable of crippling so many able individuals. The road to success and relative happiness was much clearer in the past. Now it is full of whats and ifs and insecurities. Not long ago, we believed that education and personal initiative led to job security and a rather healthy family life. But not anymore. How have we brought this chaos upon ourselves and why do we accept living like this? Do not we have any other option? All we need to agree on at this time is that so many important factors that affect our financial and emotional welfare and state of mind are out of our controls, and in fact out of the control of those to whom we have trusted the construction and maintenance of social and economic systems.

In all, the complexity, unfairness, and irrationality of social structure are making our lives too obscure and unmanageable. Making sense about this system or coming to terms with it would continue to be the most challenging task for governments and people. Yet, for recognizing 'who we are,' we must understand and defeat the effects of these erratic forces. First, we should somehow accept and cope with the fact that understanding and justifying the existing socioeconomic conditions is beyond our ability to a large degree. The intricacies and crookedness of the social and economic environments that we have inherited, and perhaps helped create for ourselves, are unexplainable and unsustainable. Why cannot we see this and do something about it? That is amazing! Second, we must get smarter and fight the temptations of getting absorbed and/or dissolved in these systems. Third, we must even find ways of flourishing as an *individual* within these substandard systems both spiritually and mentally. We must make the best of the bad situation without being pushed to despair about the whole matter of life. Handling this convoluted dilemma is quite difficult for most of us, of course. However, we must at least remember that the meaning of a person's life manifests only through his selfless and self-reliant character and not the phony social identity s/he strives to build.

Our needs and socioeconomic pressures obliterate our lives and then we blame 'life' and fate instead of social structure and our own inability to find better means of living or stopping our own role in feeding the monster ruling our world. The task of evaluating 'who we are,' both personally and as human beings, is also getting tougher with time, due to the rising personal stupidity and naivety, as well as socioeconomic limitations that one must face and cope with. Yet, we must strive for more self-discipline and spiritual power to overcome the forces of despair and confusion and to concentrate on grasping 'who we are.' What other choice do we have?

CHAPTER FOUR
Personal Limitations

We could say that life is merely a mix of our perceptions about society and ourselves. We see the values and weaknesses in society and ourselves, try to assess them, and then attempt to fit ourselves within this erratic perception of Life. A healthy society can make life feel easier and more meaningful, while social limitations make our living unbearable. The same thing is true about us as the other main element of life. Our potentialities and strengths make life easier and our limitations cause our sufferings, especially since we must face horrendous social limitations. The rise of personal limitations in line with social decline nowadays is, in fact, hindering the development and use of our potentialities, too, on top of causing us stress and depression.

Three types of personal limitations impede our own and other people's living: 1) Natural limitations, 2) Personality limitations, and 3) Self-imposed limitations. These limitations are briefly discussed in this chapter.

1. Natural Limitations (Physical and Mental)

Everybody deserves a peaceful life and a chance to develop him/herself to the highest levels of wisdom and piety in our supposedly civilized societies. This is a noble objective. However, our genetic and upbringing limitations always stand in our ways. In addition, both formal and social educations, at home and society, mislead people about the right values of life and their choices.

Furthermore, people's delusions and unrealistic expectations turn into additional limitations that hinder their ability to learn 'who they are' and why they wish to choose a particular lifestyle. Society is causing us more confusion everyday, but we also make life difficult for ourselves by our decisions.

Usually, parents have the motives to teach these facts to their children, if they were not so preoccupied by life themselves and could think rather objectively outside social norms and teachings. We all try to recognize our kids' talent, such as athletic abilities, memory, artistic talents, creativity, vocabulary and language, etc. Sometimes, teachers and other concerned individuals might play a positive or negative role too. Some objective parents succeed in pinpointing their kids' potentialities and limitations and possibly guiding them properly. Nowadays, however, most parents spoil their children with their raw value systems and their naïve intentions to maximize their kids' confidence and self-image. Thus, they ruin any chance for their kids to grasp their natural limitations and work out their options realistically. They do not appreciate the repercussions of over or under developed Ego and confidence that result from parental overindulgence of their kids. They only put more psychological pressures on their children and themselves by ignoring humans' natural limitations. They kill their spirits instead of helping them figure out their potentialities and limitations properly.

2. Personality Limitations

With our false personalities, we cause ourselves many extra headaches, mainly due to losing our identity and a chance to find 'self.' Furthermore, we attract people who are incompatible with us in terms of their needs and aspirations. Thus, we go through a long process of trial and error to finally accept that our lifestyle and relationships are only making us more depressed and desperate instead of enriching our lives. In particular, the lousiness of most relationships nowadays is due to our lack of inner power and integrity. To grasp this fundamental limitation, we must know a little about the nature and role of personality aspects. As explained in the next section, the way the three personality aspects of a person develop and manifest in society cause a great deal of limitations for him/her.

Personality Aspects

For building a peaceful life, we must work on our personalities to acquire certain personal attributes and to portray a confident image to others. Therefore, a brief review of the main aspects (characteristics) of personality and its manifestation mechanisms would be useful here.

Analyzing an individual's personality reveals three dimensions or aspects in it, which we may refer to as Self, Ego, and Model. These personality aspects are not defined here in the same context of Freud's definition of the three divisions of psyche for psychoanalysis, which are ID, ego, and superego. While the latter classification emphasizes on the way personality is developed and retained inherently mostly in our unconscious mind, the former is interested in the way personality manifests mostly through our conscious efforts. Of course, some similarities and overlaps exist between the two concepts, but the classification of the three aspects of the personality, as defined by this author, is for a different purpose. It mainly explains the way we go about making our decisions, choices, and contacts with the aid of our manipulative personality aspects.

In brief, we may say that Self is the pure, unconditioned nature of man. Self resembles that aspect of man that is defined as ID in psychoanalysis in terms of being the unconscious aspect of psyche and the source of psychic energy. However, Self is also the unexplored and underutilized aspect of a person that entails his potentialities and spirituality dimensions. Self is intended to also contain the absolute and isolated aspect of a person untouchable by negative or positive experiences of social living. Ego, for the purpose of this book, is defined to be the conditioned personality of a man that reflects his lower mental qualities, subconscious needs and desires, vanity, self-centredness and high dependence on externalities. Ego represents the self-serving needs and intentions of a person, which are mostly hidden or at least not presented voluntarily. In general, Ego is the selfish aspect of a person's personality.

The Model aspect of personality manifests in the way a person tries to adapt to social norms and in the way he presents himself to others. It often ends up becoming the main feature of his personality and who he believes to be. We perceive and/or construct one or several role models (personalities) that appeal to us. We would then internalize and behave in the form of the model that we adopt overall or apply in particular instances. We do this for the sake of satisfying our conscious needs, or hiding those unflattering aspects of our Ego that we do not care to project in our daily dealings and relationships. We also adopt a Model when we do not have a personality of our own, or when the elements of immaturity are present. Model becomes more prominent when Self and Ego are less developed and active.

Our personality is the combination of these three aspects of a person's identity at any instant. They are always present and interact constantly according to a rather fixed mix for each person. For example, an egoist is driven mostly by his Ego. Yet, the level of each aspect contributing to total personality at any point may vary and thus change a person's personality manifestation. Our mood changes also reflect the varying mixtures of the three personality aspects. (Of course, the concept of multiple personality is different from the tentative variations of personality aspects that lead to different presentation of personality and possibly mood swings, whereas multiple personality is a more permanent condition.)

Sometimes, Model may simply portray and reinforce the expectations of Ego, and sometimes Model may reflect a new feeling or role that it finds interesting and appealing. Sometimes, we can control our anger or frustration and present ourselves in a desirable format and model. And sometimes our basic honesty—a manifestation of Self—outweighs the other aspects of our personality and we say things that we might even regret later, e.g., when we tell the truth about something or someone.

Living in the highly structured and conditioning societies of the recent era has taught us to play the role of a Model extensively rather than revealing the natural person within us. That natural person (Self) is subdued and lost at a very young age anyway. We use Model a lot because we do not want to portray the deceitful aspects of our Ego, and we do not want to show our gullibility and immaturity that usually radiate from Self. And we do not have the courage to be the Self that is not favoured as an acceptable model of success and passion in our cultures.

The varying mix of our personality aspects in particular situations and times makes us behave erratically and appear moody. Yet, a person's rather unique personality manifests according to the overall prevalence of one or two of the three personality aspects. We are usually dissolved in a personality that is mostly a Model, Ego, or Self, while we apply the other two in lesser proportions simultaneously as necessary. That would constitute our main personality. *That is the personality we strive to keep happy.*

Many topics in this book reveal the direct impact of personality aspects on our lives. For example, the concept of happiness can be measured only in relation to the prevalent aspect of a person's personality. As soon as the topic of happiness arises, the immediate question is which aspect of his/her personality s/he is trying to keep happy. Our decision in this respect is crucial and determines the outcome, because the definition of happiness varies for each personality aspect. Normally, we associate the state of happiness with that aspect of personality that we are consciously giving an emphasis. For example, the happiness of Model comes mostly from popularity and approval, which does not coincide with a general description of happiness. Someone whose depth of happiness is defined to him as, let us say, having the most amount of wealth or sex has a different point of reference compared to our general impression or formula of happiness. However, even when a person is hoping to make the prominent aspect of his personality happy, his/her happiness remains shaky because the other aspects of his/her personality do not feel so happy at the same time. For example, when Ego feels happy (maybe because somebody expresses his/her love to her/him), his/her Model and Self might feel sad or even angry (maybe because s/he does not trust the sincerity of the person expressing love). These crucial factors cause extreme complications in a person's psyche for feeling a real sense of happiness. These are some additional reasons that 'happiness' remains an abstract and mythical concept. Therefore, the question is, 'How can we compare people's happiness, and how do we define real happiness?' It is almost impossible, but Part III of this book will tackle these questions somewhat.

Our genes, environment, and conscious efforts play their roles in the way our personality develops and manifests. While we cannot control the effects of genes and environment, we have some influence on the way our personality turns out, especially in the way it manifests. In fact, we often play a major role in faking a personality that is appealing and can serve our hidden and selfish needs and desires. We use different aspects of our personality randomly to achieve our immediate goals. Yet, the main purpose of our lifelong efforts to portray a certain personality is to maximize our power and appeal in the long haul. In particular, we use Model regularly in hopes of showing charisma and power. Unfortunately, however, the outcome of our efforts is usually more destructive than helpful. Many of us end up with shaky personalities that others can detect immediately, while we also keep struggling internally with the wrong self-image and a false identity that we are so keen to build and maintain. All these struggles and frustrations feel odd when we could instead use our potentialities and eagerness to create an appealing and powerful personality, which is natural too. That is, instead of trying so hard, and keep failing, to build a false personality in hopes of impressing (or fooling) others, we could direct our efforts into building a stronger inner self. By doing so, we gain the needed charisma more naturally and better than it is achievable through superficial pretences. The main hurdle that deters most people from pursuing this option is that building Self takes time, and it takes even longer for people to recognize and respect it. We are usually not patient and strong enough to wait for all these natural developments.

The main role of our personality (and the mixed use of personality aspects) is to facilitate our interactions and communications, all for the final objective of maximizing our happiness in life. We try to be assertive, manipulative, and cooperative with the use of our personality aspects in order to get things done our ways and guarantee our ongoing popularity and satisfaction. Obviously, developing the various aspects of our personalities and manifesting them in certain ways also depend on our needs, intelligence, and perceptions of people and surroundings, all for the ultimate purpose of finding happiness. Unfortunately, we have learned to nurture a set of erratic personality aspects to serve our social needs and ambitions, instead of curbing our needs and ambitions within the parameters of a natural, healthy, and stable personality. Still we hope to find happiness too! Nevertheless, the role of personality aspects on creating happiness is studied in some detail in Chapters Eleven and Twelve.

3. Self-imposed Limitations

Our erroneous judgments and decisions create a large variety of self-imposed limitations. Furthermore, we make our lives more complex and unbearable when we do not find the courage and willpower to reverse a bad decision, or at least acknowledge it. A simple example is addiction. A smoking or drinking habit may start for many reasons. A person with a good judgment would not be dragged into this position in the first place, but even if s/he were, s/he would try to rectify his/ her mistake. Some people may not be mentally prepared to fight the temptations of a habit and breaking it. Not everybody can avoid or overcome the psychological effects of some earlier decisions or failures that may linger for the rest of a person's life. This is true even when s/he feels the burdens of this limitation and understands how it prevents him/ her from developing self-esteem and a positive outlook on life.

Physical limitations due to the lack of exercise and activity, and psychological limitation due to negative thinking and experiences, are the main categories of self-imposed limitations. While the causes of these limitations may have been outside an individual, a determined person recognizes them as self-imposed limitations that only s/he can eliminate, and then look for workable solutions. Obviously, solutions are often hard to come by, while self-discipline, conviction, and commitment are needed too. Yet most of us compound the effects of our limitations because we remain passive or ignore the debilitating symptoms of our self-imposed limitations, instead of working on our willpower or seeking help.

We impose major limitations on our lives due to our attitudes and personalities. Sometimes, our false pride stands in the way of establishing or maintaining the kind of relationships we so dearly need. We may even destroy good relationships because of our egoism, selfishness, and stubbornness. At the end, we suffer personally the most from such self-imposed limitations that lead to substandard life conditions. We hurt ourselves unknowingly, because all these life burdens are the results of our naively conditioned mentality and personality. Of course, our judgments and values are mostly tainted by the outcome of our rearing environment and the influence of social norms, which means that our limitations are mainly of no fault of our own. Yet we are ultimately the one imposing it on ourselves with our passivity and negativity. We must understand and acknowledge that only we are responsible for alleviating these limitations the best we can. If we analyse our relationships, attitudes, expectations, and judgments more critically, we can pinpoint our weaknesses and limitations. Fortunately, many of these limitations are curable or controllable, if we really care to help ourselves.

Self-imposed limitations often result from the value system and lifestyle we adopt. For example, most people spend beyond their means and then suffer its consequences. They borrow money to acquire fancy clothing or pursue a certain lifestyle. Thus, they make life miserable for themselves and people around them by living like mindless robots merely following the crowd. They just let their raw ambitions and greed overwhelm their ways of building and leading their lives. They torture themselves with their fantasies, neediness, inability to find love and happiness, or thirst for power and wealth. This kind of self-imposed torture and limitation prevents us from enjoying a simple life and utilizing our potentialities. Instead, we get hung up on life trivia and superficial stuff.

Limitations Due to Missed Potentialities

While society tries to produce an acceptable level of products and services, people's potentialities are hardly recognized and utilized. Jobs get done, mostly inefficiently and ineffectively, and our efforts at best fulfil our subsistence. Nowadays, most jobs are becoming routine and automated, anyway, and often performed by incompetent, egotistical people who occupy those jobs not based on their potentialities (qualifications), but rather due to their power games and socio-political affiliations. Within such social constraints and rising crude personal needs, we hardly get a chance to *choose* a profession compatible with our primary talents and education, let alone in line with our real potentialities. The frustrating pressures of career planning, adjusting to market demands, and job insecurities, already cause us a great deal of disappointments and pain. Thus, the issue of searching for our true potentialities goes out of whack. We simply follow any means of training ourselves for the available jobs, none of which helps with nurturing our potentialities.

On the one hand, an intelligent person knows his/her life objectives and ambitions and assures him/herself that they really make sense, in some context, and for some valid ends, if destiny and luck also help him/her achieve those objectives and ambitions.

On the other hand, even if we can determine the kind of profession that matches our potentialities and temperament, we may still face a tough and major decision about pursuing such a profession when it does not offer the financial security or income level we seek. This is always a major life dilemma, because we have been conditioned to believe in a life structure that evolves around money, a career, a family, etc. Therefore, we have only limited choices in accepting what we do for a living and how it fits our potentialities. Many of us must accept this harsh reality at the end no matter how much our spirits object.

Despite the rising stress in modern societies, we usually ignore its main cause and instead get absorbed deeper in our depressing jobs and follow a bunch of shallow ideals. Our life objectives and ambitions often mislead us. Realistically, we have no other choice, while hoping upon hopes that things would improve somehow eventually. Sometimes, we run away from one employer or profession to similar or worse situations. We try to relieve ourselves from the agonies of some career deficiency and then turn around and get into an equally unfulfilling profession. Until we recognize the necessity of nurturing our potentialities and Self, we merely continue our search for different professions and lifestyles unsuccessfully—mostly for serving our Ego. All along, our spirit gets more suppressed.

The bottom line is that life feels boring and aimless for most of us quite often. Especially, the work we do feels laborious, frustrating, and stressful when not driven by worthy objectives fitting our potentialities. We may feel or pretend to be happy and purposeful with our routine pleasures and moneymaking schemes.

However, most intelligent people cannot stand the vanity of their lives without some authentic purposes for living, which usually relates to the use of their inner strengths and potentialities. When only financial needs and sense of job insecurity drive us, the chances are high that we resent the work, the environment, and often even our colleagues. Fortunately, some superficial factors compensate for the lack of more genuine motivating factors. For example, we get trapped in the games of promotions, affluence, rivalry, recognition, work incentives, and other management tools to keep our Egos amused and happy. Nonetheless, deep down we feel unfulfilled and hopeless. We feel the stress, but cannot pinpoint the real cause of it. Thus, we blame our boss's attitude, colleagues' lack of cooperation, or even family and personal problems, etc.

Naturally, the pressure to cope within society keeps us from worrying too much about exploring our potentialities to feed our souls. However, we must be sure about our choices and the cost of sacrificing our souls. In that sense, our lousy choices become another source of self-imposed limitations. We must know that not following a life akin to our passion ruins our whole perception of life. Without a chance to explore our niche in life, we feel like a soulless robot wandering aimlessly within a rigid, senseless social structure. We just imitate others and hope for the best out of the mess surrounding us. Although justified as the best means of survival, all these limitations are all self-imposed. In the final analysis, we are responsible for the outcome of our lives somewhat based on our choices.

The symptoms of our lousy choices in terms of career are evident in society as a pandemic. Seldom anybody works effectively and feels fulfilled nowadays, since our life structure and choices are limited and our occupations seldom match our potentialities. We cannot do much about the reality of life in the new era and our attempt to cope. Yet, acknowledging this common deficiency may at least increase our self-awareness, which might in turn mitigate the stress and repercussions of an unfulfilling profession.

We may admit the need to do something about the effect of this universal deficiency on our lives. We may at least look for extra-curricular activities or thoughts that activate a bit of our potentialities and mitigate work stress. Some of us may think of a side business or profession. Some may concentrate on hobbies, etc. The point is to stay vigilant of our need for some means of self-fulfilment, because our professions can hardly do that. As a rule, our professions cannot constitute (or be viewed as) a meaningful challenge of life—no matter how hard we work, and how successful our Ego makes us feel. Of course, most people do not realize their shallowness or lack of fulfillment, which is probably a way of living!

Judging the viability of a wide spectrum of our potentialities is a difficult task by itself, of course, especially when we have the added responsibility of finding only one (or at best a few of them) that appears exceptional and feels most fulfilling. Usually some seemingly justifiable areas of potentiality or professions mislead us to assume we are good at them. For example, we may think and decide that we can be a good politician. However, in reality this might have been only a premature judgment or wishful thinking behind our misleading ambitions for power and manipulating others.

In all, when assessing our potentialities and professional choices, and then throughout our lives, we should remember our reasons for our decisions. We must realize that many of our life limitations could be self-imposed because we have not assessed our choices in a timely manner within the social and emotional limitations imposed upon us. We remember that without a grasp of our potentialities and building a fulfilling career, most likely we lose our work motivation, capabilities, means of self-actualization, purpose of living, true identity, and a chance to grow psychologically. We remember that our fulfilment in life merely depends on the realization of our potentialities and not necessarily finding a high paying profession, raising a family, etc. How we then convince ourselves to live in this atmosphere of our choosing is our business. We just remember that if we cannot decide about our true potentialities, we remain doubtful about everything. Unless, of course, we conclude that we have no potentialities and are largely useless. In that case, we can focus on accumulating wealth and indulging ourselves as a way of life.

At the same time, we must remember that not building even a basic career, because we cannot figure out our niche and potentialities is even a bigger risk for our Ego, self-image, identity, and psychological health. This is a big life dilemma that we must all resolve somehow, but most of us fail.

Self-assessment

Engulfed by so many limiting factors like the ones discussed in this chapter, and pressured by normal living conundrums, such as work and family environments, drawing a true picture of 'who we are' and also nurturing our potentialities would be too abstract at best. Our efforts to grasp this blurry picture would also feel like a futile effort. However, with patience and determination, a personal self-assessment might provide clearer answers about our existence gradually. We must learn to pause and concentrate, with full attention, on our thoughts, actions, and feelings and the motives behind them. Then perhaps we plan to become someone worth being, if self-assessment shows the necessity for some adjustments, which is usually the case for all objective students of the truth. Exploring the depth of our 'self' requires more guidelines, of course, which perhaps some rational and professional people could put together soon. Probing rational individuals with objective viewpoints about life, can help us stay on a self-awareness path. Sometimes, a simple question by a child may raise a deep thought, which might eventually help answer some of the more complicated matters of life. Giving ourselves a chance to do the right kinds of thinking is the main step for earning our primary wisdom toward self-awareness and enlightenment.

The test for being on the right track becomes evident in the declining degree of our egotism and neediness. We start to see life less selfishly, in an objective and independent manner, instead of merely feeding our dogmatism or imitating the norms of the prevalent life structure blindly. We start to notice our nothingness instead of gloating incessantly about our importance. Only by gaining the capacity of doing an honest self-assessment, we become the best judge of our character and personality with fewer doubts about who we are. We may say something to others rather carelessly or callously at a moment of weakness, but would realize our error when we sit alone later for a sincere self-analysis. We also find the courage to go back and correct our mistake or rudeness, and perhaps get a chance to reconcile with people we have hurt. Our search for 'self' would still be incomplete, or not worthy enough, if we find in ourselves signs of prejudice, self-serving conclusions, unjustified parental influence, irrelevant social values, and greed. Only through a selfless, divine self-assessment, we may test the validity of our conclusions and judgments.

Naturally, being honest and critical of ourselves is difficult if we do not know how, or when we falsely believe in our sincerity. However, the worst case is when we stubbornly fool ourselves and believe to be honest when our hypocrisy is bugging even our own mind. Without an ability to control our prejudices, both our self-assessment and judgments of others are worthless. One way to test our sincerity is to recall past experiences and re-evaluate them according to their merits at the time. Do we still consider our response or reaction appropriate today, according to our new objective (rather selfless) value structure? Would a similar judgment today be valid using our present mindset and standards? Are we humble enough now to at least go back and apologize for our error in judgment and rudeness? If the answers to the above questions do not convince us that we have changed, then our effort to reach selfhood has not been effective yet. We should gauge the strength of our criteria and convictions used for assessing our reactions and judgments. We should convince our conscience (if we have one) about the rationality and honesty of our current judgments.

Self-analysis and assessment are ongoing endeavours. We become wiser by thinking more, making objective judgments, refining our value system, discussing our thoughts and beliefs with others with more care, learning more about our idiosyncrasies, and pondering the points raised in this book. Yet, some major decisions should be made at an earlier stage of our lives when we lack the wisdom we may gain only decades later after a thorough self-assessment. Relying on others for advice, such as our parents and teachers, could be risky if they cannot help youths do their own independent thinking. Thus, youths must develop and apply some quick guidelines for helping them in the early stages of their growth, as they travel through this self-disciplined learning and teaching processes.

The Final Judgment

Despite all the personal limitations briefly discussed in this chapter, we must *eventually* make a final judgment about the path of life we have chosen or like to follow. Ideally, however, we must make this judgment when we are young and have more options. While *internalizing* our ultimate limitation, death, we should always remember that life limitations compound with time and restrict what we can do and 'who we can be.' Especially our idiosyncrasies and futile aspirations should be viewed in a clearer light as we reassess their roles and significance in our thoughts and values more objectively—perhaps divinely indeed.

The main purpose of gaining a higher level of consciousness about our potentialities and limitations is to enhance our self-awareness and grasp 'who we are.' Everybody tries to deal with this dilemma intuitively according to his/her level of wisdom (cognition) throughout his/her life. However, while we passively strive to grasp our potentialities and limitations, our learning and discovery about 'self' would be evolutionary, if tangible at all. We merely wander confusedly within our infinite thought spectrum and wonder who we are. Nonetheless, this final judgment through self-awareness is important as the only vehicle for reaching a sense of contentment and maybe even happiness.

Although exploring 'self' and exploiting our potentialities are not easy for everybody, we can all learn about our limitations rather readily and benefit from our improved perspective of life immediately. Appreciating our vulnerabilities and frailties is particularly useful for earning the wisdom of viewing all other life (social) limitations with some degree of insignificance and triviality. We can then envision our life options and choose a smart way of living. Death, in particular, is a perfect tool and measure for understanding 'who we really are!'

CHAPTER FIVE
Life Limitations

Life limitations (destiny) impose many obstacles as we strive to find 'self' and unravel the power of our potentialities and spirit. Together, the social and personal limitations impede our chance of creating a simple and peaceful life for ourselves. These varied limitations affect our doubts and decisions as well, while we try hard to choose a realistic path of life. Of course, life's ultimate limitation is death, which could ironically goad us view all other life limitations in a wiser and more proactive perspective.

Life's Ultimate Limitation

Our mental and physical abilities are mostly hereditary. The bone structure, height and weight, and IQ are basic limitations, though we can influence their growth somewhat with nutrition, exercising, and learning. Despite our genetic limitations—that we must recognize and live with—, education and awareness might help a person overcome his/her personal limitations, e.g., athletic abilities or mathematical aptitude, after a long process of training and possibly revamping his/her old habits. Nonetheless, a true appreciation of one's limitations is the best way to overcome them.

On the one hand, we must envision and train our brains for their ultimate potentialities, like body builders who create massive muscles regardless of their heights and bone densities. On the other hand, overestimating our mental capacity and logic, and becoming more arrogant every day, shows our naivety. It hinders our chance for even the basic nurturing of our brains for our own benefit. Formal education per se or egotism cannot help us for real life challenges. Instead, we need to pinpoint and learn the essential means of living and relating. Learning the right stuff about life and self, including our ultimate limitations, requires patience, modesty, and special efforts, however.

Gauging our mental strengths and limitations is a natural and perpetual process that starts at a very early stage of our lives. Some basic but essential questions and realizations kick-starts the process during childhood when we become curious about our origin and wonder what gave us life, and why. What happened that we are here in this world? Before finding a satisfactory answer to these elementary but confusing curiosities, we suddenly face a more shocking fact: Death. It remains a major and stressful discovery for a few days or weeks. Then this ultimate life reality subsides after we struggle and fail to understand its purpose, even after asking all sorts of questions from our parents. Eventually, the child somehow surrenders to the harsh reality of death as he sends it to his subconscious. Every child realizes this ultimate limitation of his/her being briefly, but prefers to deny it by hiding it in his/her subconscious. Thus, our understanding of death remains at the perceived reality level, which has a tendency to be rather casual about our convictions and daily affairs. Our subconscious does not emanate the force and the meaning of death truly—as the ultimate limitation of our being.

Of course, our natural ability to forget sad realities or submerge them to our subconscious helps our sanity. However, forgetting or undermining 'death' diminishes our ability, as a child or adult, to appreciate who we are and establish a profound value system. There is a potential for initiating our self-awareness process, but we all lose this chance. Understanding 'who we are,' our inherent vulnerability, and the reality of death—that our existence may end in a second—could have helped us stay modest and alert. We could have been much humbler if we always remembered that we have no control over our most precious asset —our lives. Instead, we insist on building a pompous character and childishly brag about our importance.

The irony is that remembering our 'nothingness' regularly empowers our character and spirit. We find a deeper meaning for the things happening around us, if we remembered perpetually that our existence is really controlled by supernatural—or at least some random—forces. At this level of high consciousness, other life limitations become more bearable, and the significance of so many of our struggles for phony success would subside drastically. At this point, we graduate to the next level: We like to learn something about (or at least create a plausible imagination of) this outside force that grants us life and death. We may then decide to re-examine and adjust the course of our lives to some extent in order to play the limited role we may have in our destiny, such as not drinking and driving or eating harmful food. We would be alert about our environment and feel part of Nature and the universe. By our constant sense of mortality, we start to appreciate our existence better, and we enjoy Nature and other creatures, as we see them fragile, beautiful, but also so vulnerable like us. We try to learn from other human beings who have offered their wisdom and experiences of life. We learn how all forms of life have developed a mechanism for defence against danger and death, but also yield at the end to the powerful forces of Nature when time comes to surrender their existence. All that defence mechanism and personal wisdom would be worth not a penny.

Thus, we should celebrate death consciously as the main clue about the meaning of life, instead of pushing it to our subconscious. Repeating the word 'death' should not cause gloom either. Actually, the more we bring this reality into fore, the more we learn about the *mysteries* and *values* of life. We appreciate the triviality of all our worries and greed. For example, when a job promotion or recognition is delayed or overlooked, we would not only handle the related pains and disappointment better, but also welcome the chance to ponder our life choices more insightfully. Fortunately, many people nowadays try to keep death in their semiconscious occasionally by repeating the slogans, 'Life is too short, and you live only once.' This subtle awareness is supposed to help us mitigate our fear of taking on challenging adventures. It could also make us stronger and wiser if it were practised continuously as a ritual, and if people felt the true essence of these slogans. However, most people use them as an excuse for their laziness or carelessness—instead of alertness—or for justifying their pleasure-seeking mentality. Unfortunately, the slogans 'Life is too short, and you live only once' have become a scapegoat for people to get more reckless financially and emotionally. We always insist on missing the boat even when we get a worthy insight occasionally!

In all, while death brings us to the final frontier, it also gives us the best yardstick to gauge our lives and limitations with higher wisdom. Of course, some exceptions defy this general criterion. For example, when an old or terminally ill person suffers from pain and self-degradation, the situation could be a higher and more devastating limitation than death itself. In fact, death becomes a source of relief in this instance, too, as the only escape from life limitations.

Nonetheless, the main limitation of one's life is life itself, which is ultimately significant merely for the opportunity it renders us to trace and enjoy our potentialities, as well as the integrated potentialities of others and Nature, for only certain number of years. Even if we are lucky to have a full natural life, we should be wiser in allotting this most precious resource in a meaningful manner. We have a choice, and hopefully gain the wisdom too, to spend our lives on activities and thoughts that give us a sense of self-fulfilment and spiritual transcendence. And for some of us who have passed certain stages of our lives, it is now so clear that life is such a short journey and how ignorantly we, as a child and young adult, felt there was so much time to conquer life. We realize how we have wasted so much of our precious lives and mental energies on pursuing shallow dreams and pleasures.

Acknowledging our ultimate limitation—the finality and fragility of life itself—also gives us the proper mindset to distinguish life priorities and essentialities more objectively. The journey of life can become extremely joyful and beautiful once we discover that hidden inner power within us—our spirits and potentialities—and engage them consciously to show us what to look for, where, and how. Death, as life's ultimate limitation, could also make us realize that our inner strengths, which we energize through self-awareness, may possibly be the echo of an external force. We may attribute this external force to our creator, the God, the supernatural, or anything else that we did not feel existed before we learned about ourselves with a deeper sense of both our ultimate limitation and inner power. Remembering perpetually of our finality and fragility should become a major tool for raising our awareness and stirring the spiritual feelings that come from meditation.

A quote from Wolfgang Amadeus Mozart about death is interesting to include here, although it reflects only half of the picture of this ultimate reality. The other more important half, i.e., death as a device for putting our existence into proper perspective, is missing in his words. In fact, imagining any chance for afterlife imposes only a big hindrance to understand our existence. The idea of afterlife is just another way religions harm the naïve public and society. That is the worst manner of forgetting our existence.

> *"As death, when we come to consider it closely, is the true goal of our existence, I have formed during the last few years such close relationships with this best and truest friend of mankind that death's image is not only no longer terrifying to me, but is indeed very soothing and consoling, and I thank my God for graciously granting me the opportunity of learning that death is the key which unlocks the door to our true happiness. I never lie down at night without reflecting that — young as I am — I may not live to see another day. Yet no one of all my*

acquaintances could say that in company I am morose or disgruntled." Letter to Leopold Mozart (4 April 1787), from *The Mozart-Da Ponte Operas* by Andrew Steptoe, Oxford University Press, 1988, p. 84.

Particularly, the part he says, *I thank my God for graciously granting me the opportunity of learning that death is the key which unlocks the door to our true happiness,* is really precious.

A few other life limitations are also important to discuss briefly in the next few pages despite their lesser significance compared to death.

Timing Limitation

'Timing' (for making good decisions and doing the right stuff) is an important factor for life accomplishments, because both our personally and externally imposed limitations compound with time. For example, children learn multiple languages many folds better than adults, especially if exposed to them during infancy. The same is true for music, art, sports, etc. This 'timing' factor shows that our potentials fruit only within a certain window of opportunity. Even our extended efforts usually do not lead to positive results if we miss the timing for making the right decisions in life. This principle applies to all aspects of our lives throughout our existence with various emphasis and nature.

Obviously, our physical abilities and energy deteriorate with age. Our senses and brains lose their sensitivity and sharpness. Besides the limited number of productive years for achieving certain (and often essential) objectives, our decisions within those years must be timely too. Not a new discovery, but many of us simply forget this fact or are deluded by positive thinking gimmicks. We forget that we cannot do most things that should have been done long time ago. We should have made the right decisions when we had the chance to do so. Most importantly, however, without timely decisions, we miss life's real opportunities, suppress our potentialities, get entrapped within life's trivialities, kill our spirits, and limit our chances to succeed in many aspects of our lives later. Education and learning are obvious examples, but even simpler life decisions should be timely. On the other hand, pursuing unrealistic goals for looking proactive, or merely due to our naïve positive thinking, makes us lose great opportunities in life and look pathetic too.

Education and work constitute the primary structure of life that we automatically plan (and believe is best) for our children. However, things have not always been so structured, and even now, many children in the world do not enjoy the privileges of educational and career planning. Some are doing the opposite in fact. That is, instead of learning at the young age, they are forced to labour with no access to education. On the other hand, we may soon realize that we are keeping our children at schools and universities uselessly for no tangible benefits. It fact, we might be doing them disservice by our present policy. This principle of 'timing' must be revisited soon to ensure that both individuals and society benefit from human potentials most effectively—or at least more effectively than present. Nowadays, we are losing vast potentialities that could be better applied for personal and social benefits.

Another obvious example is the 'timing' for starting a family. Experience shows that the best time to do this is when partners have the financial resources, energy, and patience to deal with each other's needs as well as their kids', etc. Nowadays, so many auxiliary factors defer people's decision to start a family, or they raise their kids outside a family, e.g., as a single parent option. Overall, a less favourable 'timing' has become the cause of relationship problems in the new era, with no fault of people in this special case. Everybody is rightly apprehensive about the prospects of getting into a serious relationship nowadays. For one thing, partners' high expectations of themselves and each other, and the lack of mechanisms to find suitable partners, deter us from building families. The damages caused by random dating during the years prior to marriage somewhat diminish couples' ability to relate in fact. In many cases, we have to get into our second or third marriages, because of our failures in the earlier one(s)—mostly due to bad timing of various types of decisions. These assertions are not for condemning people's inability to get married soon enough, but rather to stress that our varied worries and life obligations complicate our decision to start a family on a timely manner. Thus, we get trapped in a graver mental condition. Our relationships (or the lack of proper ones) damage our psyches too. Thus, not only the matter of timing for marriage is too complex and critical nowadays, but also the effect of this delay and indecision is hurting our spirits as well as our children's.

Another example about the 'timing,' is our decision about our *purposes and interests in life* in conjunction with our careers, so that we can satisfy both our financial and psychological needs. Because of bad 'timing,' many of us end up living a miserable life due to misfit jobs and careers we get stuck with. Some people switch between jobs and careers continuously to no avail. Many of us simply choose a career as it appeals to us for some irrelevant factors, out of necessity, or wrong educational background. As an obsolete requirement of socioeconomic structure, we spend many years of our precious lives on formal education and training. Then we often decide to ignore all those efforts and hardships and train or re-educate ourselves in a different field, which usually proves unwise for new reasons. Thus, our decision about the field of education must be made at a proper 'timing,' mostly the first time, after understanding our limitations, potentials, temperament, life plans and philosophy.

Many other life situations require major life decisions. They reflect the importance of 'timing' in both our major and less obvious decisions. As a rule, though, our most important plans and decisions must usually be made at the young age perhaps before 30 or so. Understanding life and our purpose of living before making all these critical decisions is extremely helpful. However, as young people, we are only misled by social trends and propagandas instead of finding the right ways of learning about life and our divine potentialities. Thus, the outcome of our major life decisions often end up much less desirable than we usually anticipate. Our bad timing and decisions affect our families too, which then causes us indirect pressures on top of feeling entrapped in a meaningless and stressful life.

Regardless of our obsession for success and happiness, the bare requirement for health and peace of mind demands timely decisions for building our fundamental thoughts, beliefs, life philosophy, higher spirits, and a suitable lifestyle. We must make timely decisions about a path of life that is manageable with the least amount of stress.

The Meaning of Life

The meaning of life appears even more obscure within our complex social environment, even if life could supposedly be defined in some simplistic manner to satisfy our instinctual curiosity about this matter. All the social, personal, and life limitations discussed in Chapters 3-5 show how defining a meaning for life is getting more impossible with time. On the other hand, we can develop a simple life philosophy that somehow clarifies the meaning of life too. To do so, we can study the main philosophical questions that humans wrestle with all their lives.

The Main Philosophical Questions

Briefly, the philosophy of life is reflected in the three questions we ask ourselves in the three phases of our lives.

Phases of Life	Underlying Philosophical Questions
Youth	What will be (my life like)?
Middle Age	What is this (that is happening)?
Old Age	What was it (all about)?

There it is! The story of our lives as portrayed by the wisdom of our thoughts. Some precious lessons lie in this simple story. Each question may not reveal as much as they do together. They offer the gist of the deepest thoughts that engage any intelligent person as they mature. They encompass our ultimate visions, conclusions, and valuation of life experiences. Therefore, these simple questions can offer a great source of potential lessons and wisdom.

If we grasp the gist of these philosophical questions, we can set up the foundation of our thoughts properly and pursue our life plans smoothly with lesser stress. We can lay out a more meaningful life for ourselves and find a more reliable path to happiness if we remember these philosophical questions and use them as our primary wisdom.

If we are lucky to live a long life, we would surely arrive at these questions in due time. At any of the three phases, we sense and live through the corresponding philosophical questions daily, but we seem unable to find a suitable answer for them at the time. Only when we arrive in the next phase, we can see the absurdity of the question(s) in the earlier phase(s). We get a tentative and awkward answer indeed. On the other hand, if we intelligently consider the questions we would be asking in the future life phases, as shown above, we automatically get the answers for our questions today. We simply realize that all the stages of our lives would be questionable and paradoxical, no matter how hard we try to make sense out of life and how diligently we plan our actions.

For the first question, 'What my life will be like?', there is the opportunity to anticipate our most likely answers in the future phases. That is, regardless of the degree of success and presumed happiness, we would still doubt the value and meaning of our lives even when we are in the prime of our lives, i.e., the second phase. Unfortunately, the third question implies that we would not find any relief or satisfactory outcome regarding the second question either.

Of course, we are not aware of the depth and importance of the upcoming questions when we are in a lower life phase. Our Ego and arrogance would not allow it. In phase one, we do not know and believe that a more fundamental question is awaiting us, which by the way negates the importance (validity) of the first question (What my life would be like?). That is, no matter how our lives turn out, we still question its meaning and value. Similarly, we would not expect the question in phase three to be so harsh, nor expect such deep sense of helplessness despite all our wisdom and wealth. That is, no matter how much we try to make sense of life and our plans and pleasures, no intelligent person would find a plausible answer for the question, 'What was it all about?' Some radical, carefree people might resist this conclusion and insist that life is full of meanings and pleasures. Well, everybody is best capable of judging his/her deep senses and existence.

Perhaps it is in our nature to believe only in what we can feel or expect *now* regardless of all the philosophies and prophecies that are out there about life. However, for the very same reason, it seems that we waste our lives on things and thoughts that at the end would prove to have no substantive value or meaning. Throughout our lives we worry unnecessarily about things that are trivial and immaterial when we view and review them retrospectively in the future phases of our lives. This conclusion also suggests that perhaps we have all been 'living in the now' too much all along, more than what we like to admit already. That is, we judge our future needs only based on what we feel today instead of using our imagination and realize that our perception of life (according to the values of the NOW) is erroneous. We need the wisdom of foresight to make our lives simpler and stop our needless struggles and desires.

Many of us who pass through the three phases of life would admit that these three questions have hit them in a profound, and often shocking, manner. They have struggled with those questions during the whole period in each life phase. Some of us may be less enthusiastic to admit this or have lived a life of less thinking for whatever reason. Some of us may be carried or absorbed by our Egos or social pressures to the extent that thinking has been forgotten. Finally, there are those individuals who would not face these three questions, in particular the last two, because they have found a path of wisdom that directs them through the phases of life smoothly. Their life experiences are rather unadventurous, but definitely more peaceful and complete. These people have come to terms with the three questions, especially the last one, very early on in their lives.

The lessons we can learn from these questions are drawn from a projection of our state of mind and thoughts in the upcoming life phases. These questions should serve as hidden clues about the futility of submitting to the common processes and standards of life. The lesson is that, sooner or later, we would find out about the emptiness of our egotistical objectives. The lesson is that if we understand what would, and would not, matter when we are in the second and third phases of our lives, then perhaps we would aim our thoughts and actions in the right direction. The lesson is that the standard formula of happiness that our parents and society teaches us is not viable. The lesson is that perhaps we should contemplate and find a basic path of wisdom that prevents our future shocks about life's futility, to prevent our mind and energy being wasted on shallow desires and social struggles. If only we knew what we would be thinking torturously in the future phases of our lives, it would be easier for us to sort out our priorities and establish a personal philosophy that is more sensible.

We learn a lot from our experiences, except that they do not pose or answer the three main questions of life in a timely manner. Unfortunately, we do not get the opportunity to reverse past situations and conditions, or to relive the lost years. The old saying that, "Every man should have two lives: One to experience, and one to live," finds its prominence mostly during the last phase of our lives. We are willing to give up everything we have, all our wealth and worldly attachment, just for a second chance to think properly this time. We would do some (or many) aspects of our lives differently if we were given a second chance, simply because we now suddenly think differently at this late stage of our lives. Alas, we never get that chance. Alas, we hardly learn any lesson from the wisdom of foresight either.

We need a unique mentality and courage to understand and believe in the significance of the questions we would eventually ask ourselves in the future phases of life. If so, we could start *thinking forward* indeed. By thinking deep about the ultimate and eventual question of, 'What was it?' as early in our lives as possible, we can change our vision of life. We may appreciate the wisdom of this (third phase) question when we are in the first or second phase of our lives. Putting ourselves in a future state of mind is very difficult. Yet, only through forward thinking (the wisdom of foresight), we may invent an 'escape scheme' now, because in the third phase, it would be too late to escape the suffering thoughts of, 'What was it?', or the regretting thoughts of, 'What could be!' Later, we cannot do anything with these questions other than getting ourselves more depressed.

It happens that an 'escape scheme' (relief) can only be found in a path of wisdom. To become immune against the question of, "What was it?" in the third phase of our lives, we need two things. First, our fundamental thoughts should help us develop a philosophy of life by which we may assess and profess our purposes of living. Second, we must apply these thoughts and philosophy to our actions and decisions consciously and carefully in the context of *forward thinking*. This full awareness of our authentic needs and purposes in life would prevent the question of, 'What is this life?' from materializing in the second phase of our lives. We should plan properly so that we would not have to ask this question from ourselves, at least not as a lingering reality of our lives during the entire middle age.

'Forward thinking' and possible escape schemes will be discussed further in Chapter Fourteen. We intend to adopt forward thinking as a philosophical principle for developing the foundation of our thoughts and tackling the mystery of life. Forward thinking suggests that the three questions of, 'What will be?', 'What is this?', and 'What was it?' should be dealt with in a reverse order. Accordingly, we may succeed in transforming our 'perceived' world into 'real' realities that have different emphasis and significance in our lives. This approach may relieve us from the excruciating self-induced problems that we have helplessly accepted as our inevitable destiny.

'Forward Thinking' also shows that finding a meaning for life would be a useless struggle. This realization might be, all by itself, the most revealing mystery of life.

CHAPTER SIX
Life Sufferings

Human sufferings are rising mostly because our personal insecurities and expectations from life have gotten out of hand. Our societies have become too complex, while we try to adapt and manipulate others with our egotistical, shallow personalities. As all these goals hardly get satisfied, our agony and inner conflicts heighten. Our thoughts wander rampantly in vain to find a way out of this never-ending, depressing cycle.

Gradually, but much faster in recent decades, we have built an artificial, shaky life structure around vastly crooked social values that induce too much confusion and frustration. All along, this rigid structure has only further limited life's low capacity to be meaningful. Thus, only the amount of social, personal, and life's limitations grow faster every day. We try to cope with, and maybe even succeed in, this competitive, egotistical, and showy environment. Yet, our efforts to figure out life never leads to any tangible results, while we cannot stop our urges to know the purpose of our daily routines either. We just face too many disappointments due to our unyielding ambitions, people's wickedness, and our rising expectations from the vacant life *anyway*. Overall, we suffer helplessly as we get obsessed with our fancy ideologies and needs, instead of staying content with simple stuff, selfless love, and compassion.

Our needs and sufferings are usually the cause and effect of one another. Our unsatisfied needs create suffering, and our suffering induces more psychological needs, especially the need for compassion. Everybody demands a lot of attention nowadays to help him/her through the healing process or at least maintaining a minimal sanity. When we suffer, we need somebody to guide us or something to distract us. Therefore, we often end up going out shopping!

On the one hand, our neediness and anxiety create erratic thoughts, which disconnect us from reality even more and cause further illusions and pain. On the other hand, only through our thoughts (valid reasoning) we could contain our needs and insecurities somewhat. Only the right kinds of thoughts can eradicate our sour thoughts and heal our sufferings. Friendships and consoling can mitigate our pains, too, of course. However, ultimately, we must come to terms with our sufferings on our own through rational thinking. In his book, *Psychology and the East*, Art Paperback, 1978, Carl G. Jung says:

"Suffering that is not understood is hard to bear, while on the other hand it is often astounding to see how much a person can endure when he understands the why and wherefore. A philosophical or religious view of the world enables him to do this, and such views prove to be, at the very least, psychic methods of healing if not salvation." Ibid., pages 210-211.

Thus, self-awareness is crucial for enduring and curing our sufferings by grasping their sources. A life philosophy based on a profound foundation of thoughts can help the process of self-awareness, which in turn enhances our ability to think clearer and refine the foundation of our thoughts. We can even turn our sufferings into precious life experiences where inner energies and creativity erupt unexpectedly. Our sufferings often provide a chance to see some dimensions of life that remain obscure in normal states of mind. We might even unravel some mysteries of life and soothe our souls despite the sufferings caused by many normal experiences, e.g., during loneliness.

On the other hand, J.K. Krishnamurti suggests that a no-thought state can transform suffering into passion and compassion:

"When you suffer, psychologically, remain with it completely without a single movement of thought. Then you will see out of that suffering comes that strange thing called passion. And if you have no passion of that kind you cannot be creative. Out of that suffering comes compassion. And that energy differs totally from the mechanistic energy of thought." Truth and Actuality, Gollancz London, 1977, page 85.

Regardless of our success to attain the high passion suggested by Krishnamurti, we must learn to quiet our minds in a no-thought state periodically as a routine exercise for healing our sufferings. A no-thought state gives us a chance to halt all thinking and give our brains a break. Most importantly, the goal is to stop insignificant thoughts and activities overwhelming our lives and causing our sufferings. However, we must first learn to distinguish between significant and trivial life issues and how to use the former to defeat the latter. This means that before entering the state of no-thought or meditation, we should decipher the causes of our depression and suffering, as explained in Chapter Twelve. Only then, we may maintain a no-thought state where the healing can become complete and permanent.

Our suffering intensifies when we cannot grasp its source or insist on creating foolish rationale for it. Often we create some imaginary reasons or excuses to justify our suffering and our feeling of self-pity, perhaps hoping to attract other people's sympathy too. All along, we only inflict more sufferings on ourselves for no reason other than the weakness of our convictions and souls, and sometimes out of laziness to take proper actions for getting out of our self-imposed mental slump.

We humans have a tendency to doubt or deny the causes of our suffering instead of admitting that our stress is a symptom of a widespread social problem, i.e., the vanity of our lifestyles. We often ignore our inner feelings (conflicts) that signal the real causes of our suffering or quickly turn them into the feelings of defeat, self-pity, and uselessness. Sometimes, we deliberately suppress our thoughts and the symptoms of our hidden problems, e.g., neediness or greed. Sometimes, we allow some elusive concepts like love and happiness deceive our grasp of reality. When we doubt our inner feelings and instincts about our suffering, we dampen our interest or motivation to adjust our approach to life and living. Not knowing our real reasons for living, or adopting erroneous purposes, causes our sufferings too. We are often too stubborn to accept the fact that our shallow mentalities are causing all our suffering, and instead keep pushing the same values and methods that have proven impractical and stressful. A good example is our absolutely erroneous approach in marital relationships and still continuing with the same methods and expectations. We cause our own sufferings through our idealistic and whimsical thoughts.

We all have personality issues and psychological defects, which create pain and problems for others and us. These personal idiosyncrasies, however, differ according to our unique needs, interests, and willpower. The healing can begin only when we stop doubting the fact that our peculiar defects and obsessions are causing most of our sufferings. We must acknowledge our paranoia and hang-ups, and learn how to view, defuse, and cure them. We need the courage and commitment to overcome the main barrier, i.e., our denial of the depth of our insecurities and eccentricities. We have some lingering doubts about our identity and purity, but fail to stop and analyse them.

We must admit that nobody out there in society is going to change to accommodate us and reduce our sufferings. The chance of finding our soul mate or even a reliable companion is also quite low. The odds would not rise if we keep imagining otherwise or dreaming. We must learn to accept, and live with, all these painful facts of life. Actually, we should expect the matters to get worse and pressures to mount in the years to come. We must accept the hard reality that no one understands and cares about our sufferings and real needs the way our imagination desires. Life hardships would hit us all our lives with very limited, if any, compassion.

Life struggles mount when we refuse to adjust our expectations, mentalities, and attitudes. Or when we deny the reasons behind our sufferings, which are mostly self-induced—often due to our naivety about the meaning of life. Or when we do not try to ignore those insignificant life events and expectations that stir our erratic thoughts and break our spirits. A list of common sources of sufferings and related discussions are offered in Appendix 6A at the end of this chapter.

Enough clues are around us about our misunderstanding of life. We must use them to enhance our self-awareness instead of ignoring them. Our frustration and anxiety often reflect our inattention or misinterpretation of the causes of our suffering. We feel helpless because our struggles do not bring us relief. Instead, we feel desolate and lonely, and we get more exhausted and stressed out every day with our search for love and happiness. We try to correct the whole world and to make everybody understand our concerns. We like to inform our friends and family about our failing relationships and neglected needs. However, it seems, the more we try, the less we succeed to communicate with the rest of the world. Our frustrations and anxieties keep rising and we look in the wrong places for remedies. Yet we refuse to reassess our value systems and adopt a simpler lifestyle. We naively believe we have already figured out the meaning and purpose of life.

Another problem is that we look externally for the causes of, and the cures for, our sufferings. We look for the faults of others, things, and systems. We ignore that mostly our own defects, and our persistence to take the perceived world too seriously, produce our sufferings. Our ignorance of our inner powers inhibits our real potentialities to surface and energize our existence, while our thoughts and primary wisdom also lack a strong foundation. Grasping these concepts is difficult for a person who is trying hard to find an honest job to meet his financial obligations, but keeps failing due to discrimination or job shortages. But if he finds the wisdom of living in the real world, realizes his inner powers, and looks for his few real needs instead of many superfluous ones, then perhaps he would stop caring too much about finding a job altogether. He learns to create his own job, accept a lower paying job, or maybe even ponder the possibility of living without a job if he has the psychological power and resources to do so. The bottom line is that *ideally* not even joblessness should become a cause for chronic stress and suffering. It must *ideally* induce more creativity to explore other options and opportunities for living.

The mere acknowledgement of our defects and the causes of our sufferings would most likely mitigate the feelings of frustration and helplessness already. Then this awareness helps us to subdue these known (deep-rooted) causes of sufferings gradually. Only we can adjust our mentality and adopt a more practical life philosophy. We can change our lifestyle and attitude to subdue our sufferings, and maybe even remove our personal defects and desires causing them.

We can build a profound foundation of thoughts upon personal experiences, through studying the visions and prophecies of great thinkers, and by making a finer judgment about the truth of existence. We can weed out the influence of social conditioning on our thoughts and our power of reasoning. We can refute common ideas and perceptions that are senseless. We can resist the temptation of living and thinking for external approval, sexuality, greed, and power—as they are the direct sources of our sufferings. We can learn to manage our pains and paranoia better by pinpointing the insignificant thoughts behind them. And we can refuse to comply with superfluous standards and expectations propagated in society.

Common Sources of Suffering

Although we have unique personal reasons and remedies for our sufferings, most of them have common sources. Learning about the nature of endemic social sufferings can expedite our awareness and lead to faster recovery. Of course, the nature of suffering and its intensity varies according to individuals' sensitivity, insecurities, weaknesses, surroundings, and outlook on life. Nevertheless, the common sources of mental sufferings relate to some kind of personal needs deprivations, such as:
- Financial burdens and worries
- Social burdens, sexual deprivations, and loneliness
- Paranoia, greed, jealousy, spite, etc.
- Psychological defects and chemical reactions in brain
- Lack of social recognition, insecurities
- Personality imbalance due to excessive Ego or Model
- Stress, fears, physical issues, unfulfilled dreams, etc.
- Incomplete or problematic relationships
- Lack of self-actualization and spirituality
- Boredom
- Etc.

Often a few of the above sources mix and cause niggling thoughts and a feeling of mental suffering. The fact that our sufferings are creations of our thoughts does not mean they are not real. Yet their intensity is based on our perceptions (thoughts) about their importance, causes, and effects. Remembering this fact and controlling our thoughts help us mitigate our sufferings, mostly by redefining our purposes of living. Furthermore, solutions are found easier for most of these causes if we unlearn the conventional methods and criteria of assessing our problems. We must become a bit more creative in circumventing social inconveniences and pressures. What we perceive as a problem might not be a real issue at all in a new perspective. Of course, suffering is mostly an emotional reaction, which is hard to measure quantitatively or set a rigid criterion about. Normally, our minds evaluate a recent situation in reference to past experiences or erroneous expectations (as a criterion) to gauge its intensity. Our conditioned brains do some tricky and hasty assessments before we start to feel the suffering. Thus, we must discard the patterns and directions of our conditioned minds, and instead, depend on our awareness to assess the causes and effects of a recent painful experience in a compassionate manner.

Recalling Mozart's comment on page 61, he seems to have grasped some personal visions about life beyond normal comprehension, perhaps as a source of his ingenuity, too. In fact, we believe that some people are blessed with a better sense of life and an ability to turn their insights into precious notions. Fortunately, we have benefited from their insights too, though not enough, because most of us grapple with so much unnecessary sufferings, despite all the knowledge and culture our ancestors tried to leave behind for our enlightenment.

Meanwhile, we also wrestle with some cynical observations about God's role in our sufferings. For example, we wonder how richer our lives could have been if geniuses, like Mozart and Chopin, had not died so young or suffered so much, like Beethoven, merely in pursuit of basic life privileges such as love. On the other hand, we wonder about God's wisdom when the ingenuity of *at least* some blessed humans goes to waste or dies so quickly, while the wicked, greedy tyrants thrive universally and ruin commoners' chance for even a basic existence. How does this prevalent criterion for the 'survival of the fittest' provide any kind of support for God's benevolence? What can we deduce about God's love for His privileged creatures? Can anybody imagine the possibility of unravelling any of these life mysteries?

Still, we wonder about the meaning of life when deep down we believe love is the core of life and the main key for exploring life's mysteries. Yet true love is nowhere to be found—maybe not even in the God's design of the universe. Why? What is love?

PART II

Love

CHAPTER SEVEN
The Nature of Love

Love has turned into a big obsession for humans, especially those hypnotized with the high delusions of modern societies. Many reasons exist for this phenomenon. Obviously, our instinctual urges and mounting psychological needs play a major role. Our new social values, including the effects of mushy movies and deprived sentiments, have also confused our impression of love and our handling of this myth. Love appears like the main source of happiness and the main attribute for defining our lives. Accordingly, it is now also considered the most important factor for the success of relationships. Overall, we have not only contaminated our impressions of love and life, but also caused more headaches for relationships in the new era. Therefore, studying the nature of love is necessary for resolving some of the ambiguities clouding its meaning and capacity. In particular, we should learn about the role it can realistically play in relationships. After all, the highest application for love is its role for choosing a companion and gauging the viability of our relationships.

Love as a Reflection of Personality Aspects

As noted in Chapter Four, people's personality has three aspects with the following characteristics:
a. **Ego** reflects (and drives) our desires, ambitions, sense of responsibility, defence mechanism, and all other traits that enable us to assert ourselves and protect our lives.

b. **Self** contains our inner urges, selfless love, integrity, inquisitiveness, potentialities, creativity and spirituality. This aspect of our personality reflects humans' soul and vulnerability.
c. **Model** is the most practical aspect of our personality in the way it tries to help us adapt to social norms and get accepted and admired if possible. It is driven mainly by our conditional and adaptation needs.

The above three personality aspects also perceive, and react to, 'love' differently. The spiritual love (SLove) that we often perceive and long for arises from Self. We have an instinctual desire to love an idol that we imagine in our minds. Usually this basic force instigates our search for a soul mate. We remain optimistic all our lives to find such a person despite our negative experiences in relationships. Our initial attraction to someone triggers our naïve Self, and we feel romantic and hopeful about his/her attributes. As a simple, optimistic creature, we quickly see perfection and find many reasons for adoring him/her unconditionally. Then our actual experiences and interactions with our partners begin to disprove our initial perceptions and hopes. Therefore, we begin to impose our desires and fantasies upon our partners and demand that they behave in the way we had mentally pictured them. When they do not—because they cannot—we get mad at them and ourselves and show our frustration even more. We continue pushing them to become the idol we want them to be, or we decide to abandon (maybe even hurt or kill) them for their imperfection and disobedience. In either case, our Ego makes these love related decisions and triggers our sense of possessiveness. It acts with utter arrogance, despite Self's struggle to maintain the initial love image and to continue satisfying its thirst for SLove. Ego is the personality aspect that is now *demanding* love. We just want to feel loved because of our Ego. Let us call this type of love as ELove (Ego driven love). When neither Self nor Ego can succeed, eventually Model emerges to put a stop to the inner fight between Ego and Self. It tries to impose equilibrium. However, we eventually get tired of our efforts to change our partners or stabilize the relationship. Some of us might finally give up our dream of finding (or creating) a soul mate, or even maintaining a friendly relationship with that particular partner. We submit to our doomed destiny. We might continue to live with a person we no longer love. We have no stamina or motivation to fight anymore. Model, as the adapting agent, takes over to a large degree in hopes of keeping some kind of civilized love relationship (MLove) between partners. Some sentiments of Self and anger of Ego continue to distort the equilibrium that Model is trying so hard to maintain. Eventually, we often learn to adapt and live through our Model, with some degree of MLove. It can help us cope with bad situations and learn tolerance.

In general, our Self's needs, especially SLove, are seldom satisfied in relationships, although our Ego and Model often make us believe otherwise. For example, some people believe that they are happy and loved in their relationships, because their Ego and Model give them that impression. Some people are aware of humans' true nature and thus keep their expectations from their partners in check. Some people are too self-absorbed to care about their Self's needs or their partners' love for them. Many people try to satisfy their Self's needs in other passions outside of their relationships, e.g., in art or nature. In all, most people do not find SLove in their relationships. Therefore, they either try to validate their relationships in some practical ways without SLove or keep looking for love elsewhere.

With Model, we hide our true emotions and anger about our partners. Sometimes, Model helps us show love, too, which, despite its artificiality, feels pleasant to our partners at times. Sometimes, it even feels satisfying to us. We begin to perceive and enforce an illusion of love (MLove) in our minds in hopes of mitigating our need for SLove. This delusion helps us carry on with our lives, while deep down we might feel awful for being illusive. Nonetheless, our culture advocates the use of illusive love to sustain our sanity and our relationships. We try to pretend

MLove through Model to remain tactful and to validate our relationships. This is a practical approach simply because finding SLove is a rather unrealistic goal for most people. So now, we have the following types of love:
- **SLove** is Self driven and reflects the most **spiritual** and selfless way of loving someone. This is what Maslow refers to as B-Love.
- **ELove** is Ego driven and reflects our **deficiency** need for love and attention. This is what Maslow refers to as D-Love.
- **MLove** is Model driven and reflects our most **practical** way of communicating our passion to another person.

These notations for love are used in the remainder of this book. Each of these three types of love satisfies one aspect of our personality. On the other hand, it must be clear that not all three types of love can be satisfied simultaneously, although we need or crave a good mix of them together rather regularly.

Overall, it appears that relationships might thrive better if we stop considering SLove an important factor. That is, maybe we could allow a more practical definition of love be driven by Model instead of Self. We do not need to see love a selfless and exaggerated devotion, but rather a means of respect and harmony. This (MLove) would be a practical definition of love for the new era, which is driven by Model. It might actually work. This point will be further discussed in Chapter Ten under the heading of *The Power of MLove*.

The Meaning of Love

How does the commonplace expression of love fit the notion of SLove, ELove, and MLove? It seems that the commonplace love consists of i) attraction, and ii) a mix of SLove, MLove, and ELove. This theory confirms the following facts:

- A person's 'need for a companion' is driven by all the three aspects of his/her personality, and each personality aspect plays a special role when he/she expresses love to another person.
- Seeking love reflects both our instinctual and conditional urges.
- Each person is driven by various levels of SLove, MLove, and ELove when expressing passion. Thus, the meaning of love is different for each person depending on the level of each personality aspect he/she applies to perceive love. The intensity of love also varies based on his/her insecurities, needs, and the prominence of each personality aspect. Moreover, his/her level and meaning of love change rapidly, too, in different circumstances, even toward the same individual.
- Inventing an imaginary meaning for love (anything other than for defining SLove, ELove, and MLove) and spreading it for common use is pointless—except for writing fiction and making movies.

Overall, when we fall in love, all aspects of our personality exert a type of love that we wish to fulfil. If someone is totally selfless and willing to give love without condition, his/her SLove is most prominent. However, for most people, their urges for romanticism and spirituality are only partially triggered by some perception of SLove and physical attraction. Behind their idealism for SLove lies their need to fulfil their love deficiencies, i.e., ELove. They also play the role of a good lover by applying the charm of Model to impress their partners through tender expressions of MLove. Usually, their initial impression of SLove fades away after they get into relationships. The reason is very simple: People who are not driven mostly by Self cannot maintain SLove. SLove and Self go hand in hand.

SLove also diminishes when new perceptions about our partners soon override the initial ones. Therefore, the majority of us end up perceiving love and handling it in a personal, and unique (non-SLove) manner. If we are patient and properly trained, we might be able to bolster our relationships by using only MLove. In most cases, however, we end up nurturing only ELove in our relationships and put unreasonable demands on our partners. Meanwhile, we expect our partner to love us with his/her power of SLove. We want him/her to keep proving his/her selfless love. What an Ego!

The inherent nature of love, particularly the effect of human hormones, shows that love does not survive too long in relationships in the form we had initially perceived it. What we call love nowadays is often only a combination of lust, possessiveness, and insecurities we have compiled through social interactions and imitations. Accordingly, love cannot be a main success factor for relationships either—not even SLove. Only couples' ability to relate and their capacity for compassion, comradeship, integrity, teamwork, as well as their knowledge of the relationships' specific needs can stir sincere passion and prolong their relationships. Successful couples eventually learn to create that sense of attachment and compassion without depending on SLove or ELove. With people's increasing need to be self-reliant, couples would gradually adjust their mentality about the limited role of love in relationships. Then they can seek both love and relationships realistically without assuming that they are necessarily the same or the cause and effect of each other.

Couples may even wish to substitute the word 'love' with some other word that conveys their commitment and understanding of relationship responsibilities better. We could actually create a word to express love in relationships, such as MLove, e.g., by saying: "I mlove you." It means, 'I like to cherish you realistically based on mutual respect and teamwork, and I will try to respond to your needs for compassion the best I can.' It does not sound too awkward to pronounce 'mlove' either. If a person were certain and courageous enough to say I slove (SLove) you, it means that he/she is willing to devote him/herself to his/her partner and he/she does not even look for love in return necessarily. He/she does not even mind being a slave for his/her SLove.

Now we can be clear about the meaning of 'I love you.' Although most loves are ELove in relationships, nobody would admit it. In addition, only a few people may have the courage and conviction to admit that they SLove their partners. It would be such a big commitment. They cannot take it back lightly if they say to their partners that they slove them unconditionally like a slave.

Therefore, the most likely type of love people would express to one another would be MLove. Very clear. They stay practical by expressing a kind of love that is conditional on partners' attitude and ability to share MLove. However, the good thing about MLove is that both partners realize that their love expressions are not exaggerated emotions, but rather a conditional and calculated message of affection. Couples could actually express their attraction to each other most often by using the phrase, 'I'm attracted to you' instead of using the word 'love.' Moreover, when they wish to use the word 'love', they might like to be specific that it is only a sense of compassionate and practical MLove. Hopefully, we might eventually minimize the need for ELove in modern societies. If we can at least eliminate the ambiguity of love from relationships, we would be taking a giant step in the right direction. The word 'love' creates an ambiguous picture in partners' mind that is neither practical nor real.

Of course, there is no harm in using the word 'love' as an expression of intimacy as long as we remember its true meaning. Indeed, with the frequency we express love to one another all the time, it is losing its traditional inclination gradually anyway. We are learning that it should not be taken seriously. Therefore, introducing Mlove and understanding its purpose, as a substitute for the corny expression of love nowadays, would serve relationships tremendously. Anyway, it will help couples to distinguish the three types of love as noted above and understand that we usually express ELove, or at best MLove, to each other to fulfil our need for compassion.

Somehow, many people imagine that their partners have really meant SLove when they expressed love and maybe even cried for each other during some romantic moods. This misperception causes confusion and places unreasonable expectations on relationships. Usually, a person's emotional expressions, including weeping, are only the symptoms of his/her 'desperation for a companion' and a reaction to the existing chaotic environment of relationships. He/she is tired of looking for the right match and someone to soothe his/her agonies. Do not take it as SLove.

People's Impressions and Expressions of Love

We exchange love (mostly ELove) to satisfy many personal needs and motives. Some of these motives are:

- To *communicate* with our partners. Showing passion may be only a means of striking a conversation with our partners for many reasons, maybe for measuring some aspects of the relationship, or possibly even for manipulating our partners.
- To express our basic *feelings*. We may show passion to draw our partners' attention to our urgent needs and feelings. We may feel happy, fulfilled, depressed, lonely, lost, etc. We like to share any kind of feelings with our partners and hope to receive their sympathy too.
- To release *psychological* pressures. We may show passion for satisfying our needs for acceptance and dependence. Insecurity and need for continuous recognition motivate a partner to use ELove as a mechanism to enforce his/her dependency on his/her partner.
- To mimic our *spiritual* needs. We have an instinctual urge for SLove. Although our medium range needs prevent us from acting on this high-level need, SLove is triggered subconsciously now and then, e.g., when we hear a romantic tune or

watch a drama. For a moment, we get in touch with this obscure feeling, i.e., SLove. We may eventually act upon it, but usually these spiritual experiences are fleeting moments that we cannot internalize and apply regularly. As noted before, SLove happens only after fulfilling (or containing) our basic and medium needs and becoming a needless and selfless person. This spiritual love requires high levels of maturity and enlightenment.
- To *control* our partners. An inconspicuous, but common, purpose of love is to satisfy one's need for control. That is, often, a person's urge for love is for the purpose of controlling his/her partner somewhat easier. People exchange love phrases, hoping to enhance their partners' love for them, so that they can live within certain boundaries agreeable to one or both partners, depending on who loves the other more and who is setting the boundaries. People's rising urge for control is not always out of malice. They do it because that is the only method they know for managing their relationships and for prolonging them. Another reason for partners' 'need for control' is that they trust each other less every day and thus get an urge to impose controls on each other.
- To *manipulate (abuse)* our partners. Sometimes a partner expresses love or attachment only for (ab)using his/her partner—mostly for his/her personal needs—mostly financial and sexual needs—with the least amount of sincerity in his/her words or attitude.

A side comment worth making, based on the above discussions, is that both our basic need for sex (including the urge for reproduction, especially for women) and our high-level need for love (SLove) are instinctual needs. Therefore, it appears that we have created most of the medium-range personal needs through evolution and according to cultural conditions. As we have felt psychologically weaker and more vulnerable within new environments, we have developed all types of superficial needs to soothe our suffering and deal with our dependencies on others. We have also introduced new social values and personal games to satisfy our urgent need for a companion. This is another clue that the faster our societies grow, the more superficial needs we impose on ourselves and our relationships, and the more complex the relationship environment gets.

The above noted motives drive us to use the word 'love' rather sloppily. In the absence of a better word to express our exact motives (or just for hiding them), using the word 'love' for so many purposes has become customary. However, it is important to keep our expectations from exchanging 'love' phrases in proper perspective. Surely, the word 'love' covers a large variety of meanings and none of them really reflects true love (SLove). Also, note that love is perceived and applied differently by each person according to his/her psychological and circumstantial needs. It has no definite meaning to draw upon or set expectations for. We can apply it arbitrarily only to soothe our need for compassion without making an issue out of it or expecting long-term commitment on that basis. "You said you loved me!" is a common complaint when couples interpret love based on arbitrary and ambiguous perceptions.

The Importance of Defining Love

Two crucial impressions about the virtues of companionship drive our love urge: First, we are programmed, instinctually and culturally, to look for a soul mate because we believe he/she can relieve our loneliness and complete our identity. Second, we have come to believe, logically and scientifically, that a good companion can *potentially* satisfy a wide range of our personal needs, including sex, compassion, and spiritual (selfless) love. In a sense, we intuitively put too much faith in the vast potentials of companionship. And we spend a lot of time and energy, all our lives, to find that special person who matches our image of a soul mate. Anytime we meet someone resembling that image, we begin to fantasize about him/her in a 'love routine' to test our luck with this new candidate.

Accordingly, the word 'love,' in the context used nowadays, consists of people's impression (and expression) of their 1) urges, 2) feelings, and 3) moods during their search for a companion.

The **Urges** that drive humans to find a mate are Sex, Compassion, and SLove. Compassion is meant to include other urges such as ELove, security, dependence, respect, recognition, etc.

The **Feelings** related to humans' search for a mate are numerous, including delight, elation, lust, jealousy, possessiveness, hatred, anger, and almost all other feelings that humans face while chasing any desire. A variety of feelings emerges during couples' love affairs and separations.

The **Moods** that emerge during humans' search for a companion consist of: Attraction, Romance, and Attachment. They are fed by a mix of urges and feelings, but also by conscious assessments. That is, we use both our instinctual and logical attributes to manage these moods (processes or modes) successfully. These three moods, i.e., attraction, romance, and attachment, are close reflections of our urges for sex, SLove, and compassion respectively and they are satiated with a huge amount of feelings too. We also use our logical and calculating minds when we are in one or more of these moods. These moods reflect a person's state of mind and the progress of a love affair (all for the purpose of fulfilling his/her need for a mate).

Attraction is triggered by physical appeal, lust, but also our careful evaluation of a person's attributes and resources. Our instinctual criteria for selecting a mate, mostly for bearing a child with this person, often play its role too. People (and love literatures) usually confuse attraction with love. The minute they are attracted to someone, they believe they are in love.

Romance is our innate impression of SLove and our calculating expressions of passion (MLove) in order to lure in our beloved. Therefore, again, we are using both our instinctual and logical assets to find a companion and satisfy our ELove need.

Attachment is the effect of closeness to a person and enjoying the compassion satisfied by this union.

'Attraction' has always been an instinctual mood (process) for selecting a mate throughout the evolution. However, it has been a temporary mood just to bring two naturally suitable couples together. Nowadays we get, or pretend to be, attracted to someone based on many unnatural factors, too, such as his/her wealth, status, or our own personal insecurities. So, attraction nowadays has become even less stable.

'Romance' has always existed in nature in some form, too, although its role has been tentative for animals and humans. Nowadays, however, we humans like to have a lot of it. And since romance is only partially intuitive (the impression of SLove), we have to fake a lot of emotions not only to impress our beloved, but also keep them impressed enough to stay with us. This is an added pressure on relationships in the new era—a naive demand that is raising couples' expectations and tension.

With respect to 'attachment', scholars believe that it has evolved in humans as the need for support to raise offspring emerged for our ancestors many millenniums ago. It was mostly a temporary arrangement, too, and then partners went their own ways when children could live on their own. However, nowadays we have gotten used to the idea of having a long-term commitment with a partner. This mentality has grown stronger because of humans becoming more insecure, religious, and needy for love and compassion in recent centuries. Of course, we have at the same time become more arrogant and choosy and thus sabotage our chances to sustain long-term commitments with anybody. Nonetheless, our yearning for both romance and attachment appears to be largely self-imposed moods and also a reflection of humans' insecurities as well as struggle for social morality. The upcoming discussion of love-related human hormones will show that we are not built to be romantic or stay attached to one another for too long.

Many feelings, including elation, lust, hope, security, dependency, etc. emerge when a person's urges (sex, compassion, SLove) push him/her to find a companion. As love *moods* progress successfully, or when they face disappointments, more feelings are still brought into this situation, such as the feelings of possessiveness, jealousy, hatred, anger, depression, suicide, etc. We have historically combined all these urges, feelings, and moods and called it love. We not only confuse love with attraction, but also attach a large assortment of feelings, urges, and moods to this initial attraction and call the whole mix 'love.' That is why love has always been a vague definition and too difficult to deal with. People suffer because of love for two main reasons: First, the forces behind their love urges, feelings, and moods are not clear to them in order to deal with the sources of their anxieties directly. Second, they assume love is a lasting condition. Thus, they feel defeated miserably once they face the natural downfall of love. They take it too personal, while cursing their beloved too.

Need for a Practical Love Perspective

Understanding the true meaning and implications of love might help us curb our initial unwarranted enthusiasm and prepare ourselves better for its heartbreaking consequences. Therefore, recognizing the moods, urges, and feelings related to love is important.

The first thing to agree on is that the customary method of combining all the *urges, moods, and feelings* related to 'finding a companion' and calling this overwhelming mix 'love' is confusing, but also untrue. The *urges, moods, and feelings* related to 'finding a companion' should be studied as psychological reactions—symptoms of love—but not love itself. They are the same symptoms that manifest at lower intensity when we have any desire, e.g., for a car or a pair of shoes, especially when satisfying it falls outside our means. This is a fine distinction, which its usefulness will be explained shortly.

So what is true love? True love is that unique instinctual urge that we have identified as SLove. Love, in its purest sense, is just a simple, selfless appreciation for the mere 'being' of another person without having any selfish urges to own, control, or impose one's needs upon that person. Just pure SLove as a unique state of mind. Most people have experienced SLove temporarily when they have been affected by music, nature, their children, some kind of passion, or during self-actualization. This pure feeling of SLove, which is engraved in our unconscious, is occasionally directed toward our beloved, too, but usually for a short period. We fail because we cannot internalize SLove unless we learn to become a selfless individual. Anyway, in real life, we create all kinds of images and love moods (attraction, romance, and attachment) in our minds when some flickers of SLove strike us. However, these love moods are only the outcome of our pressing urges for 'sex' and 'compassion,' while we struggle to find a companion. We encounter all kinds of feelings, including sexual attraction, security or insecurity, dependency, passion, jealousy, possessiveness, attachment, ecstasy, etc. The minute these varied emotions are introduced in any love affair, SLove loses its inherent property and love becomes something totally different. It mainly turns into ELove.

Overall, it is our strong 'need for a companion' (once directed toward a particular person) that creates all those urges, feelings, and moods that we customarily (and wrongly) attribute to love. 'Love' does not create all those (good and bad) feelings that usually leads to enormous suffering (despite the initial elation and hope). "So don't blame love," is one important conclusion to draw here. Only our deprived 'need for a companion' causes pain all our lives. This simple and subtle distinction is important because it makes us reflect inwardly to put our love related urges and feelings into a proper perspective. It would help us remember that our powerful 'need for a companion' and 'sense of loneliness' often make us behave in strange ways. The induced symptoms are unrelated to love or our beloved. The real cause of our restlessness and loneliness is not love (or a lack of it), either, although we crave more love the lonelier we get. The real cause of our loneliness is our increasing inability nowadays to *relate* to one another, while our obsession to find a soul mate keeps growing at the same time. This awareness might help us redirect our focus to ourselves and become more objective. Instead of self-pity, we could act smarter about our need for a companion. We might decide to adopt a new mentality: to either give less importance to having a companion, or go about finding him/her in a more honest and productive manner—unlike the present approach, especially the emphasis on love along with a large assortment of game-playing. We would also learn about the true meaning of love (SLove), compared with the selfish manner that we have come to define love nowadays.

Our 'need for a *dependable* companion' is actually so impaired it has turned into '*desperation* for a companion' in recent decades. As noted before, a companion can *potentially* satisfy a large number of our personal needs, ranging from sex to compassion and SLove. Our instincts and social conditioning make us see these deceiving potentialities as real possibilities. That is, we remain hopeful all our lives to find a soul mate who would fulfil most of our personal needs. But our chances for actually finding a soul mate is quite remote, and then realizing the 'potentialities' of a companion is even smaller for all the reasons explained in various books by this author. Nowadays, partners have difficulty even fulfilling each other's basic need for sex on a long-term basis, let alone all those more complex needs for ELove, compassion, and SLove. Therefore, while people never give up their optimism about realizing the potentialities of relationships, their real experiences keep leading to failures, frustration, desperation, and anger. People's chronic optimism is admirable but corny.

Confusion about the Meaning of Love

Our confusion about the meaning of love and our 'desperation for a companion' would keep rising every year, because we cannot find or keep a partner or trust him/her in the long run. Obviously, this critical state is the outcome of drastic social changes and our rising idealism. Instead of understanding the roots of relationship problems and our role in causing many of them, we keep dreaming about a soul mate and an ideal relationship with another partner. We do not see the futility of our search for love or a soul mate. With more relationships failing every year, we get more desperate, which, ironically, only heightens our craving for both passion and compassion even more. In all, our obsession for love nowadays is a reflection of our increasing loneliness and desperation for a companion, while our exaggerated expectations (including love) ruin our relationships and we become even more desperate and lonely. This vicious cycle is destroying people's trust in each other and their expressions of love.

If we look inwardly to review our personal needs and relationship expectations objectively, we can find the roots of relationship issues and see how they are causing havoc in society. Then, instead of blaming love or a lover, we might focus on changing our mentalities about love and relationships. We would understand why finding or keeping a companion has become so difficult nowadays. We would then realize that love cannot be the success factor for relationships and thus redirect our focus to our own personalities, lifestyles, needs, demands, and methods of finding a companion. The way we have become—so haughty and needy—is to be blamed for the failure of relationships, not the lack of love or couple's inability to be romantic.

Love has always been studied as a combination of many feelings, urges, and moods related to humans' search for a companion. Following some rudimentary methods, scholars have defined many types of love based on the categories of those feelings and urges. It is true that love leads to, and stirs up, a mix of all those urges and feelings, but it does not mean that love is all (or a portion) of those feelings and urges. The way various types of love were defined two millenniums ago, based on the symptoms or the object of love, is still pursued by some scholars at the present time. If the ancient Greek had defined ten different kinds of love, now psychologist come up with six or eight types again based on its symptoms. For example, psychologist Robert Sternberg suggests that love has three ingredients, i.e., 1) passion, 2) intimacy, and 3) decision and commitment. Then he defines seven types of love based on a mix of these ingredients. For example, he suggests that *romantic love* is a mix of the ingredients 1 and 2. *Infatuation* is 1 alone. *Empty love* is 3 alone. The other types of love are *consummate love* (1 + 2 + 3), *compassionate love* (2 + 3), *liking* (only 2), and *fatuous love* (1 + 3). Maybe the next question is the proportion of each ingredient in each mix! (Also, notice that love and relationships are used synonymously in his method, as evident by the definition of *empty love*.)

Dividing love into certain categories according to certain feelings would not help the chaos in relationships. It would only convolute the meaning of a simple concept like love. For example, identifying *romantic love* as if its true nature were different from other kinds of love (if it contains any real love at all) has very little practical implication. The only important question is whether this romantic love has any sense of SLove (selflessness) in it or not. If yes, how? And if not, should it be even considered love, romantic or otherwise? In the final analyses, the essence of love is always that notion of selflessness toward another being regardless of all the feelings and urges exerted in that particular case, e.g., love toward our children, parents, a person, or even objects such as nature, an artistic passion, etc. Love is always the unique feeling of SLove regardless of all the emotions that get attached to it. Having (or showing) compassion is noble and perhaps even more precious than love, but it is not love in its true sense; it is compassion. We should continue to distinguish passion from compassion and respect each category of feelings attached to them separately. More importantly, the symptoms of love should not change the nature of love, if it were true love. Hundreds of love symptoms emerge in different situations according to people's personalities. Bringing them into a definition of love causes only ambiguity about the meaning of love.

We make a big fuss about the way a lover becomes restless, jealous, depressed, sleepless, etc. However, these symptoms are common in many other situations, too, when any particular plan or desire of a person is threatened. People lose sleep or become restless about any matter that occupies their minds, e.g., a project, a catastrophe, etc., or get jealous if a job promotion is given to another person. Of course, love-related symptoms are usually more intense than other cases—only because of our 'desperation for a companion.' However, those symptoms do not define love.

In the end, there is only one kind of love (SLove) that can be directed to any person or object when it is sincere and true. For practical purposes, we must then focus on approaches that can help us find and relate to our partners easier and build manageable relationships. One objective of this book is to switch our focus from 'love' to 'need for a companion,' which is a term more akin to 'relationships' than 'love.'

It is acknowledged here and in other parts of this book that getting hit by love is an extremely powerful experience and dealing with its symptoms is very difficult. We feel all those mind-blowing urges, moods, and feelings related to this so-called love. We cannot change the fact that we keep falling in love and we must deal with its symptoms. So, one could argue that maybe it seems easier to attribute all these symptoms to one simple concept, i.e., love, for our common communication. This might sound like a reasonable proposal to people. They would probably prefer to view love that way: surrounded by all those ambiguities. That is fine, if they really prefer it that way. That is at least fine for making movies! However, it is essential to recognize that none of those symptoms (urges, feelings, moods) has anything to do with pure love.

Pure, unselfish SLove satisfies some peaceful emotions and urges of humans, but it does not lead to self-destruction or war with our beloved. This would be the simple definition of love that is adopted in this book. Hatred, retaliation, and rage, when love fails, clearly show that our perception of 'love' had not been pure (SLove). Obviously, many of our selfish and destructive urges and feelings influence our *impression and expression* of love. And it helps to know the real motives behind these urges and feelings.

In all, people's sense of love nowadays consists of their mixed urges for sex, compassion, and SLove. Then they express some feelings and moods while pursuing their goal to find a companion. Research has shown that people's sense of love might last maybe up to two years, but it is usually shorter. In addition, research indicates that humans' mating moods, e.g., sexual attraction, romance, and attachment are not necessarily directed toward the same individual constantly. We are chemically (instinctually) built to connect to different people for satisfying different urges. Various hormones that drive our moods for love affect one another to a large degree as shown in the next section, but often they work independently to allow humans to be in several relationships at a time. We are already witnessing the outcome of humans' true nature (especially sexuality) as it is manifesting freely in our modern societies. This is not a very comforting situation for building long-term relationships. But this is the reality of life, another mystery, at least for the time being.

The Effect of Hormones on Love and Relationships

The hormones that rule human urges do not seem to support people's excessive expectations from love and relationships. The recap presented below is the author's overall understanding of various research findings in the field of human hormones. These findings can hopefully help us more in the future for building relationships. Meanwhile, they reveal some interesting points

about the effect of human hormones on love and relationships. These findings are not absolute, but seem to match our daily experiences, too:
1. Testosterone is the hormone that increases the urge for sex.
2. Vasopressin and oxytocin are hormones believed to cause the urge for attachment.
3. Testosterone, vasopressin & oxytocin exist in both genders.
4. During orgasm, vasopressin increases in men and oxytocin increases in women. Therefore, **sexual activity seems to increase partners' urge for attachment.** Especially, after-sex cuddling seems to be the result of these hormones.
5. Vasopressin and oxytocin also trigger testosterone. Thus, **attachment hormones could enhance sexual urges.**
6. However, if the dosage of vasopressin (and possibly oxytocin) is increased, the level of testosterone is reduced. This implies that **prolonged attachment might reduce partners' desire for sex.**
7. Testosterone can trigger vasopressin and oxytocin in animals and most likely in humans too.
8. However, increasing testosterone dosage would reduce vasopressin and oxytocin and thus dampen the urge for attachment. This implies that **too much sex might diminish partners' desire for attachment.**
9. Dopamine is the chemistry for romance. It is the hormone that triggers passion, attraction, and ecstasy.
10. Dopamine and norepinephrine might stimulate oxytocin and stir attachment under certain conditions. This implies that **romance sometimes leads to attachment.**
11. On the other hand, no definite relationship has been established between neurotransmitters of romance and the hormones of attachment (vasopressin and oxytocin). Thus, **romance and attachment are not proven to be related**.
12. In fact, oxytocin interferes with dopamine and reduces its effect. That is, the **attachment hormones can suppress the romance hormones.**

13. Increasing dopamine reduces the level of testosterone. This implies that **romance diminishes the urge for sex.**
14. Some DNA of a gene causes monogamy in some animals and also in the laboratory tests on mice. Some people have a trace of this DNA, but not all humans. Therefore, **no chemistry or evidence has been found in humans to suggest they are built to be monogamous.**
15. Various studies have shown that **love usually dies between six months to about two years.** Of course, some people have continued their love under certain conditions based on their unique personalities and definition of love.
16. Research shows that **humans' mating moods, e.g., sexual attraction, romance, and attachment are not necessarily directed toward the same individual constantly.**

To summarize the above findings, we can safely blame human hormones for the following facts:
- Sexual activity triggers the mood for cuddling and attachment, but the increased sex might erode the sense of attachment in the long run.
- Although attachment might increase sexual urge, prolonged attachment might eventually dampen the urge for sex.
- Romance and attachment are not proven to be related.
- Attachment might erode romance.
- Romance might erode sex.
- Humans are not built to be monogamous, unlike some animals that have the right chemistry for it.
- Love dies most likely within six months to about two years.
- Humans are chemically (instinctually) inclined to connect to different people for satisfying different urges (romance, sex, attachment).
- The effect of human hormones and mood changes, especially for women during childbirth, menstrual cycle, and menopause, contribute largely to gender differences.

The effects of hormones on our behaviour in a sense suggest that we should not really feel too guilty for being so sexually inclined and losing our willpower to honour our wedding vows and relationship commitments. They also suggest that we should not get too mad and frustrated with our cheating spouses, either, if we could logically see their helplessness about all these tricks of Nature. On the other hand, we cannot stop wondering about humans' ability to be a bit more ethical and have some level of self-control, despite all their natural tendencies. What kind of society and relationship atmosphere we humans really need and can support?

CHAPTER EIGHT
Misperceptions about Love

The lengthy discussions in the previous chapter reveal our gross misperceptions about love and the prominent role we expect it to play in our relationships. The evidence of this epidemic in society is everywhere around us. Particularly, in recent decades, couples have suddenly become too romantic, but also too antagonistic. Everyone believes that love should be the foundation of relationships. In this sense, life has become a big theatre. Everybody tries to be romantic. And they expect their partners to be equally good in romance, too, as a test of their commitment. But then, they retaliate harshly, and show their evil side, when love fades away—which happens regularly in most relationships. They turn separation into such a calamity when they realize that their supposedly initial love had been a farce. They make life hell for themselves and their partners because love has evaporated (if there had been any real love to begin with). Now couples turn into ferocious adversaries accusing each other of lying about their earlier love promises. They curse their partners for not loving them anymore, as if love were something to force upon oneself and not a natural phenomenon. They find their partners responsible for the lost love, even if they are the ones feeling out of love. Actually, they often blame their partners for making them fall out of love. They accuse their partners of having killed their love. They also blame them for their loss of youth. These past lovers now suddenly view each other as criminals deserving a severe punishment, including a difficult and costly separation. The penalty for falling out of love is too horrendous nowadays. Therefore, some people continue to play the role of a romantic fool to keep the situation under control. They accept the humiliation of submitting to the whims of their spouses to stop their whining, and because the penalties, financially and emotionally, for ending relationships are too high. Nevertheless, most of us still feel obliged to be romantic, just to keep up with social norms and expectations.

Almost everybody finally admits that love, in the sense they had initially imagined it, is a transitory state. Then they may decide that the option of staying in loveless relationships, against their convictions, is preferable to loneliness or high penalties of separation. However, now they do not know how to handle a relationship that is not defined by love. They believe their relationship has failed and has no value. Some may seek love in another person's arms; to find the love they believe they deserve.

Everybody believes he/she deserves love and must find it somehow. However, we all ignore a simple fact about the meaning of love: That the more one seeks SLove, the more one must be honest and sincere in character. Yet, it is becoming more difficult to be honest and sincere nowadays, because of all the games introduced in relationships. Of course, we imagine that we can hide our insincerity, mistrust, and dishonesty from the rest of the world. However, this mentality only shows our arrogance and trust in Model to bail us out. The good news is that people can largely see each other's true nature despite all the elaborate games they play to portray a false personality of themselves and to conceal their calculating nature. In all, the games and retaliation schemes in relationships show how ridiculous the idea of measuring the strength of our relationships by love is. We just ignore all these contradictions and keep looking for SLove in such a contaminated environment.

Nevertheless, many of us face a big dilemma: On the one hand, getting out of relationships proves excruciating, in terms of the hardships imposed by our partners and society (the judicial system in particular). On the other hand, many couples are frustrated and confused, nowadays, because they feel trapped in their loveless (usually hostile) relationships. The situation is in particular stressful for persons who really believe that love is the essence of relationships. Even worse, many couples have to continue playing some phony roles that marriage counsellors tell them to play in order to save their relationships.

Our present mindset reflects our lack of clarity about the nature of love and its role in relationships. Overall, we insist that relationships, and its survival, must be justified and driven by love. In the contemporary definition of relationships, our culture permeates many invalid myths. We believe that:

- Love is the test of relationships' success.
- Love lasts forever.
- Love makes a relationship last forever.
- Relationships must be validated by love.
- Relationships thrive on love.
- Anybody considering a serious relationship should and would find a person to exchange love with each other.
- Expressing love regularly guarantees relationships' success.
- Love is a common phenomenon that everyone understands and is capable of delivering.
- Love is a common commodity that everyone must find and enjoy in his/her life.
- When there is love, relationship problems are rare and manageable.
- Love overcomes all the relationship problems.
- Partners can control their feelings to love each other forever.

These myths are furthest from the nature of relationships in the new era. Love does not have the meaning or the power stipulated in the above myths. Nor do relationships necessarily last longer if partners start their relationships with love. We are not learning any lesson from the fact that almost all relationships in the modern world have started based on *some kind of love* and they still keep failing miserably. It is amazing.

Maybe it is all right to seek love so eagerly. However, we should also remember the nature of love in general—as outlined in the previous chapter—as well as the chaotic nature of relationships in the new era. We should do so to be prepared for the consequences of our futile search for love or even after finding it. We should indeed concentrate on developing our Self (selflessness) instead of indulging ourselves with more ELove and phony lovers. Besides, SLove happens by accident and not active search.

Another cause for misperception in relationships is that partners use love as another yardstick for measuring equality. That is, they expect their partners to love them as much as they think (or pretend) they love their partners. They demand love-equality to ensure the fairness of their relationships. Obviously, love-equality is a symptom of the general equality craze in society. People believe that love is a spiritual feeling (Self driven), but then make it totally conditional on their partners' ability to love them equally. With their demands for ELove and equality, they simply expose their selfishness (instead of selflessness) and destroy their chances to relax and relate naturally.

Couples' perception and expression of love are obviously not SLove as long as they insist on love equality. It is even more bizarre when they often retaliate harshly when they do not perceive the love they get adequate. How can this attitude have any trace of SLove in it? It is at best only a Model driven love (where partners try to play the role of lovers), without any sense of selflessness (needlessness for equality). This is clearly an example of partners' increasing confusion every day about their perceptions of love, which then leads to more expectations from relationships. The need for equality has become such an imposing social phenomenon that it has even infected our love affairs and relationships. We are less interested in figuring out how our partners' integrity may qualify them as our soul mates. Nobody knows what the characteristics of a soul mate should be. Rather, we insist on measuring, in greatest accuracy, the equality (as well as the intensity) of the love our partners can show, which we continue to doubt anyway.

While equality, in the sense of *fairness,* is the foundation of our democratic society, it has turned into a socio-political platform to further spread our demented social values. The term 'equality' is somewhat misused inadvertently to express our repressed anxieties, which then leads to creation of new expectations and headaches. Unfortunately, the meaning and implication of equality are often exaggerated, so much so it has ruined the structure of relationships altogether.

In fact, relationships' chances of survival have declined drastically with love becoming the main success factor—because love itself cannot survive in relationships. Actually, a cynical interpretation of *love* implies that it flourishes only by deprivation and not through a relationship. Perhaps believing that relationships (marriage) kill(s) love is cynical. However, we can safely say that after the initial stages of companionship, couples encounter a special atmosphere dissimilar to their initial perceptions of *love*. The new atmosphere is shaped according to the peculiar personal needs and personality aspects of partners, which is hardly ever spiritual or logical. So, in light of all these clues, both a more meaningful view of love and a better perspective of relationships are needed. The question is why should not our culture focus on factors that are effective in prolonging relationships without depending on love too much? And the question is why we cannot identify these relevant factors of success for relationships? The answer is that we really do not appreciate the true nature of love and relationships in the present era. And we have not yet realized the importance of developing a relationship framework.

Many of us might realize eventually that our perceptions of an ideal relationship are unrealistic and then lower our expectations. We may end up thinking *practical* at the end, but not before hurting ourselves and our partners for a long time with our misperceptions. Often it would be too late anyway. 'Practical' is mostly a reference to a type of submission, 'a sense of resignation and disappointment,' that eventually prevails in relationships nowadays. Most relationships contain good doses of resignation and disappointment. On the other hand, many people may lose good companionship opportunities due to their unrealistic demands. They destroy their marriages or look for an idol until most of their useful lives are wasted on dreams. Some of them might then further damage their pride, integrity, and convictions when they keep downgrading their expectations drastically for the sake of getting into a relationship quickly despite its obvious flaws and predictable headaches.

CHAPTER NINE
Love and Loneliness Dilemmas

Of all our needs, belonging and love have the strongest mental impact on our lives both positively and negatively. They are medium range needs on Maslow's personal needs tree, but are emerging nowadays quite urgently as deeply psychological attachment needs. Considering the fact that our needs for food and security are somewhat attainable and automatic in modern societies, love and belongingness needs occupy our minds and psyches the most all our lives. In that sense, 'search for a companion' manifests as a basic human need, since we all crave it so intensely and passionately and yet often fail to satisfy it properly, if at all. Finding the right companion makes the biggest impact on our psyches, as it balances our emotions and life outlook permanently. Companionship provides great happiness when it is successful, but it causes extreme pain and disappointment when it is loaded with arguments, failures, and separation.

The health of relationships is also an important factor for maintaining the socioeconomic welfare of any nation. In modern countries, in particular, the deteriorating social condition makes the study of relationships extremely urgent and sensitive, mostly as a *basic* personal need, but also a complex social phenomenon. Accordingly, this author's comprehensive book, *The Nature of Love and Relationships*, provides a full picture of this critical topic. The discussions in this book are rather brief, merely for highlighting love, life, and happiness as the main topics of concern for individuals in the current era.

Love and loneliness are major life dilemmas for almost everybody, because we seem helpless in choosing a viable option for living and loving. We do not know how to relate effectively, but are not trained to live rather independently either. Instead, we are fed with all sorts of fantasies about love and filled with the fear of loneliness. The effect of our dependency on organizations and society weakens our spirits and we hope to find refuge in a companion. Yet, love and companionship needs result in an even higher level of dependence and desperation.

Right after earning our sense of independence from our parents, we find ourselves in need of loving and being loved. Sexual drive intensifies and complicates the matter even further. Therefore, before we really get a chance to test and enjoy our independence, we get drawn into other deep sources of dependence, like love and companionship. We feel our need for dependence even before we actually meet somebody or build a relationship. The mere sense of loneliness and need for companionship weakens our whole image of being and freedom. After we meet somebody and actually start a relationship, the level of dependence increases even more. While trying to cope with, and nurture, our feelings of love and dependence, our inherent need for individualism, as an independent, assertive person, also keeps imposing another set of deep inner conflicts. Furthermore, our struggles to distinguish, consciously or subconsciously, between our love needs and sexual drives become an added source of confusion and doubts.

In all, our desire for independence and our inevitable submission to our urges for love and sex turn into major dilemmas throughout our lives. We struggle all along to solve these dilemmas by fixing (and balancing) our feelings somehow, helplessly and uselessly. While we have more feelings of control and independence during some periods, we soon revert to our need for love and the feeling of loneliness (the need for dependence) that comes with it. For either love or sex, or simply eluding loneliness, we have to depend on somebody else who is willing to share similar feelings or experiences with us. Our relationships require mutual dependence and understanding in order to stabilize. Without some degree of commitment and integrity, relationships do not last or take the form that would satisfy our need for a companion. All these requirements create a major paradox in our existence.

Our ceaseless cycles of need for dependence or independence cause psychological shocks, and lead to depression. For one thing, we start to doubt our identity and 'who we are.' We doubt our understanding of love and companionship and we doubt the effectiveness of our approaches to find and manage them. We start to doubt our ability to judge and decide about our preferences and options on this matter, and about our ability to be an independent person. We get entangled between our emotions and logic fighting forever. Yet, our doubts would be a blessing under the circumstance, because dogmatic logic or mushy emotions could cause even more mayhem, including the chance of forcing hasty decisions. Nevertheless, the sense of helplessness in decision-making and our stressful doubts during the perpetual cycles of dependence-independence are not easy to deal with either. These natural, conflicting personal feelings are painful, while we face the rising headaches of relationships in society and couples' inability to relate nowadays despite their deep needs for a reliable companion.

Marriage and companionship are the biggest source of lingering doubts in life, because both options of living alone and with someone else cause us pain and stress nowadays. Sometimes, loving someone makes us feel even lonelier when we cannot relate to him/her effectively and often feel unappreciated and helpless. This never-ending source of doubt and stress is a reason why marriage has become a major life decision. Our warranted doubts and cynicism about relationships, and the effects of dependence-independence cycles, reflect the deteriorating state of relationships and the growing complexity of our basic need for love and companionship. The vast scope of relationship issues is best evident from the ongoing frictions and problems in our own or other families and the rising percentage of marriage failures. In all, the level of deficiencies and deprivations caused by love and loneliness nowadays make the topic of relationships quite sensitive and important for individuals and society as a whole.

Loneliness Dilemma

The loneliness dilemma erupts from our conflicting sense of desolation both within and without a relationship. We feel lonely without a good companion and we feel even lonelier in our relationships that are often so dysfunctional. The severity of this dilemma rises from the fact that we cannot do a damn thing about it personally. It can possibly be resolved only in a relationship and *only if* two people learn to relate and thus eradicate their mutual sense of desolation. So, the importance of redefining our relationships becomes obvious for resolving loneliness dilemma for more people.

We like to have a companion with all the qualifications that our Ego and ELove seek so selfishly. We want a perfect companion to satisfy our needs for dependence and companionship, but we also love our individualism, while unable to overcome our personality flaws and idiosyncrasies either. Therefore, we feel lonely even if we happen to be in a reasonably peaceful relationship. Our obsession for love and happiness, and our frustration for not finding them, also cause havoc inside us.

Nevertheless, the dilemma of loneliness is hard to overcome until 1) we learn about the inevitability of feeling lonely all our lives, and 2) grasp the real causes of relationship conundrums in the new era. Only few people can resolve loneliness dilemma by maintaining good relationships nowadays, until a new relationship framework becomes available in society. Thus, our main option to partially resolve our loneliness dilemma is to learn the art of leaving independently and lonely for the most part of our lives. This requires developing a personal life philosophy that pushes more self-reliance and the pursuit of happiness outside love and relationships. Meanwhile, since we all prefer to have a companion anyway, we must also try to change our mentality about love and relationships and learn to tolerate a most likely imperfect partner for the rest of our lives. All these mental adjustments and self-awareness are hard to undertake.

Hopefully, the society as a whole would soon embark on creating a useful relationship framework for couples to relate more effectively in order to resolve their loneliness dilemma somewhat. Explaining the process of developing a new relationship framework to solve the loneliness epidemic is beyond the scope of this book. However, just as a primary effort, let us develop two lists: 1) A list of irrelevant desires and motives that preoccupy us and overwhelm our relationship decisions adversely, and 2) a list of useful factors in line with the right purposes of relationships. For a stronger commitment, such as marriage, we should be even less flexible and sloppy in terms of choosing the relevant success factors than in the case of a simple cohabitation.

The Role of Relationships

The importance of love and our eagerness to unravel the mystery of love is due to its presumed role for relationships' success. Now that we know more about the nature and meaning of love, we must focus on finding better means of 'finding a companion' and building good relationships without relying on love too much, if at all. Love is important, but building healthy relationships is even more essential nowadays.

Certainly, life is more beautiful and tolerable when the outcome of our decision about a companion is positive and we have a peaceful, pleasant life with a person whom we deeply care for and understand. A compatible and cooperative partner brings the most gratifying experience for a normal person with average intelligence. Conversely, if our decision turns sour, which seems to be most likely nowadays, the repercussions are often too extensive and destructive. Decisions about marriage normally result in one of these extremes, although some couples learn to live peacefully together despite their conflicts and differences. These facts seem to be obvious and common sense. However, for whatever reasons, most of us fail in our decisions. More than fifty percent of marriages in North America lead to divorce. And another great majority of couples live separately or desperately in substandard relationships all their lives with no guts to get out of them.

The role of relationships on the quality of our lives is quite important, while we naively take love as the main factor for the success of our relationships. Thus, understanding the role and needs of our relationships is an urgent mission for getting a better control of our lives.

Our *needs* for sex, love, and compassion constitute the natural motives behind relationships. Furthermore, our cultures and ethics demand that we engage in some formal ritual to make relationships binding and dependable. The purpose of these rules is to protect individuals, enhance family values, and strengthen the nucleus of social structure. All along, we have learned to expect a stable relationship (preferably a marriage) with a person we have spent a lot of time to find and tame. On top of all these natural and cultural motivations, however, nowadays partners have grown high expectations from relationships in line with their mounting personal needs and dreams. These new needs, especially partners' craving for love and attention, have risen drastically in recent decades and thus making the task of relating in relationships difficult. People are obsessively looking for happiness, which they believe comes mainly from love and relationships. However, this is a bizarre expectation—to make our partners responsible for bringing us that illusive happiness that we seem incapable of finding on our own. We ignore the fact that since nobody can find that elusive happiness, expecting it from one another in a relationship is pure silly. The relationship environment has also become too complex as people have become more selfish, greedy, and unreliable. While they seek deep love and lasting relationships, they are losing their sense of commitment to cultural or general family values. No new guidelines exist either to at least provide the basic rules of relating in relationships and keep partners' Egos manageable. So, people get into their relationships with crooked motivations and idiotic expectations. While they have become oversensitive and obsessed with finding love, they have little compassion and patience themselves. Under this confusing situation, people settle for a companion for all the wrong reasons without any knowledge of relationship needs or even a true sense of love, though they naively consider 'love' the main success factor for building their relationships. Accordingly, they also get out of their relationships with equally selfish motivations and hasty decisions in pursuit of better companions and more sexuality. People often seem to get married according to their calculating minds and agenda while misperceiving or ignoring the real purposes of relationships.

Overall, it is becoming difficult to assess partners' (often-crooked) personal motives for starting a relationship beyond the natural needs of humans (for a companion). Thus, a keen assessment of our motives (both our own and partner's motives) is required before making a decision or committing ourselves to a binding relationship. Obviously, all these doubts and decisions have incredibly high consequences on the quality of our lives, either positively or negatively—mostly negatively, though, in the new era.

If we think we are so smart when we are making our marriage decision, then why are most of us failing? It seems that we are wrong in our decisions because:
 i) We are unaware of the purposes of marriage outside our superficial attraction to another person and our idiotic, high expectations.
 ii) We do not analyse, or ignore, our own or partner's motives.
 iii) We do not know enough about relationships' unique needs and the individual we are planning to marry.

iv) We are not familiar with the harsh realities of married life beyond our limited observations of our parents and perhaps some friends or relatives.

Simply, we do not know what we are getting into. More importantly, no longer any reliable norms and guidelines exist for partners to use for planning and maintaining their marriage, while their extreme Egos and misperceptions keep increasing their expectations from relationships. In fact, we do not even take our parents' experiences seriously, as we think we are immune to their types of mistakes and problems.

It is interesting how much time and energy we spend on simple decisions, such as buying a pair of shoes. Especially women endure a big dilemma to stay rational, considering their obsession for shoes nowadays. We assess its quality, our need for it, where we are going to wear it to, price, etc. We wish to justify our decision logically (because we have to pay for it) instead of emotionally (simply because we like it). Yet, considering the lifetime consequences of marriage, we do not study the right factors and our motives properly or at all. When it comes to love and sex or the presumed benefits of marriage, we often lose our sense of logic and foresight. We are fooled by the mirage of marriage too prematurely. We feel too lonely to worry about the reality of relationships. By the way, humans' long list of obsessions for a variety of objects and whims, e.g., women's obsession for shoes, reveals the inherent irrationality and carelessness of humans in assessing their real needs and purposes. Driven merely by our obsessions for love and happiness, false emotions, or financial incentives, we forget to study the needs and complexity of relationships adequately beforehand.

In fact, we have not learned how to define and study the relevant factors of relationships' success. Considering the magnitude of marriage decision, we do not spend nearly enough time to learn and apply proper criteria to measure marriage variables and situations. Heck, we do not even have any guidelines and criteria to use these days anyway. Of course, we take a lot of time supposedly thinking and evaluating our options and decisions. However, our hesitations and doubts about marriage or selecting a companion do not necessarily mean that we are studying the matter logically. We are not really aware and informed of the right factors to study, anyway. Especially during the courting period, we are overwhelmed with thoughts and emotions that are more distracting than helpful for a true assessment. We usually get swayed by our love and sexual needs; we believe we should compromise; or we ignore or undermine our preferences, purposes, and intentions. We do not give enough weight to the importance of this decision, because we are unaware of the repercussions of bad marriages, which is almost an epidemic nowadays. Often our motive for marriage is merely to change our monotonous lives, often in hopes of escaping other sad realities of life. Sometimes, a partner views marriage merely a means of financial security. In another case, a person lowers his/her standards of an acceptable spouse because s/he is getting old and perhaps her 'biological clock is ticking' too fast. Thus, we jump into a marriage carelessly, hoping that it would work out fine. Marriage is certainly a big change, but as statistics show, it is usually a change for worse.

Irrelevant Factors and Purposes of Marriage

The most commonly misperceived reasons for marriage or a serious relationship in the new era are:

Love Need: This is a strong and beautiful need that we crave permanently, but often at the expense of a lifetime misery and disappointment. Everybody is misled by mushy movies that show how love makes people's life eternally beautiful and happy. 'Love need' occurs in three ways. First, we crave being loved per se, like a psychological deficiency. Second, we imagine and believe that we adore a particular person and cannot live without him/her. Third, we superficially build an image of love that we believe a person is offering us, which we usually accept out of loneliness, desperation, or our innate urge to love or be loved—and thus we replicate the feeling of love. None of these love criteria is directly relevant for building a serious relationship. The more obsessed we get with this need, the lonelier we normally feel.

Security and Dependence: This factor is against the basic principle of self-reliance and self-image that we value so much nowadays. Starting a partnership in a weak position would not help any relationship in the long run. Insecurity puts demands on both partners. The spouse who requires special attention and a sense of security would most likely be disappointed after marriage to find out that his/her spouse does not care or cannot provide the extreme attention that is demanded of him/her. So he/she feels too lonely. The spouse pressed for special attention eventually gets fed up with his/her partner's abnormal demand and withdrawals from the relationship.

Financial Gain: It is needless to discuss the immorality and irrationality of planning personal gains as a purpose of marriage or companionship. Yet, many partners bring their calculating nature to relationships nowadays.

Convenience: One or both partners consider marriage a means or matter of convenience, financially or emotionally. Sometimes, they marry just for changing their monotonous life routines. Family and cultural pressures to build a family often lead to these types of marriages too. Marriage is used as a scapegoat, while partners remain oblivious of its enormous potential for causing major headaches, frustration, and inconveniences of its own, instead of solving their initial problems. Focusing on personal problems and inconveniences, which partners hope to eliminate through marriage, often reflects their ignorance of relationships' peculiar needs and capacity. They do not realize that in fact they should get ready to fulfil many curious roles and expectations just for the sake of being in a relationship.

Relevant Factors and Purposes of Marriage

Three relevant purposes exist for marriage outside the instinctual needs to mate and have a family. They should exist simultaneously for making a positive decision about a particular marriage. These purposes (motives) maximize the interests and welfare of two intelligent individuals who view marriage as an institution or partnership.

Increase Life Enjoyment: Marriage provides the opportunity to explore life jointly in a more significant manner. Obviously, sex, love, and compassion are expected to prevail and provide enjoyment, especially during the early stages of our lives when we need all those good things the most. However, sharing experiences in general and doing certain activities together intensifies partners' enjoyment of life extensively as well. Life's inherent values become more vivid and meaningful when they are jointly appreciated, while partners express their feelings and interpretations. Just the mere opportunity to have someone around to discuss, or complain about, things gives couples a warm sense of relief if not enjoyment. Married individuals have a longer life expectancy, mostly because they can share their joys and anguish. They get a chance to share their hurts, mitigate the effects of external pressures on them, and get back into happy mood cycles faster.

Support and Cooperation: Marriage should provide a suitable environment for cooperation and teamwork to solve problems, and to strive for higher personal achievements. Partners' joint participation in household and family affairs leads to better results and a higher synergy with less energy wasted by each partner if they lived alone. More importantly, partners are expected to support each other functionally and psychologically in order to grow, think clearer, and stimulate a variety of communications that would be creative and thought provoking.

Sensible Commitment: The ultimate purpose of marriage is companionship. However, while 'companionship' remains a romantic and natural notion, 'marriage' comes across as a contractual obligation of partners for a joint venture. We do not think and feel as much romance when we talk about marriage, as it is inherent in the meaning and purpose of companionship. This subtle expectation of romance fading with marriage is, of course, a realistic vision based on what we subconsciously know and observe in most marriages. Our negative direct experiences and general observations in society have created a dubious perception about marriage. It appears, particularly, that men are more reluctant to commit themselves to marriage, partially to protect their independence and partially due to their higher apprehension about married life and its inevitable anguish—perhaps because they have less maternal incentives that goad women more naturally and forcefully.

It seems as if with marriage we expect the innate purpose of companionship lose its steam eventually in spite of partners' unparalleled initial love and romanticism. Accordingly, marriage seems more like a scheme to keep partners together even under situations not tolerated in a non-committal companionship. Although we are not naive to assume that problems of alienation can be resolved by making separation difficult through marriage arrangement, we believe that some simple formalities (like the ones we now have) can protect us from the situations where our agitated Egos explode and we make hasty and regrettable decisions. Through marriage, we are forced to learn and practice some common sense in making our relationships work instead of keep searching for an ideal mate forever. After all, ideal couples can be found only in fairy tales. Nowadays, however, couples are unaware, or ignore, even this basic purpose of marriage, i.e., a sensible commitment.

In marriage, we may eventually learn that stubbornness and false pride only lead to alienation and separation. We expect the loss of some intensity and passion in companionship over time, but hope to acquire the wisdom of comradeship to accept and adjust to our partners' imperfections. These same imperfections would have separated partners if they were not married, and had not learned the means of overcoming their stubbornness and false pride.

Therefore, marriage has a special purpose that makes it distinct from a simple companionship. We may call this a 'sensible commitment' to make a relationship work if it is logically possible. However, most of us are not acquainted with this purpose of marriage, or do not work on it consciously as a major requirement of marriage. Contrary to full commitment that many naïve partners dream and expect from their marriages, 'sensible commitment' is conditional upon partners' ability to relate in many respects *in order to develop* a natural sense of commitment when hardships or conflicts arise. The *sensible* commitment grows naturally when partners learn to relate peacefully and respectfully, instead of expecting a blind *full* commitment egotistically. Our common view and concept of marriage is an incomplete picture, which we have learned from our parents and movies. We have never had an opportunity to understand the real purposes (and shortcomings) of marriage before we get into one. And once we are in it, we do not know how to assess and respond to complex situations prevalent in modern relationships. We either suffer through it too much too long helplessly or run away from it prematurely, based on our emotional and arbitrary criteria for tolerance.

CHAPTER TEN
The Mystery of Love

The main objective of exploring love in Part II has been to challenge its importance for relationships' success. However, love remains a haunting reality for most of us forever. Despite our arrogance, flaws, and lessons of failing relationships, love continues to overwhelm our lives like a heavenly impression, a myth, a craving, a helplessness. Therefore, some kind of a reality check about the mystery of love and humans' compelling romanticism is necessary. After all, most people seek romance instinctively, and then become even more helpless when they eventually face it. We simply inflict more misery upon ourselves by our obsession for love; as if God has deliberately forced such a horrendous punishment upon humans to counterbalance the joy of love that He bestows upon them occasionally. We are driven to fall in love and then pay a high price for its bliss in the way lovers torture each other. The situation is quite frustrating because we, such intelligent creatures, cannot decide between the heartache of being in love or the suffering of a loveless life. By the way, the question of being in a relationship or not (with or without love) is a different dilemma all by itself—separate from the headaches of love altogether.

Our lifelong struggle to find love or suffer because of it is becoming more prevalent in the new era. On the one hand, economic growth is giving us more time and money to spend on our social needs. On the other hand, the high stress from social chaos and our dashed ambitions make us more susceptible to fall victim to love, or at least an impression of love, which has even harsher effects. Be it a reflection of our instinctual, social, or psychological needs, love is such a beautiful and yet hurtful phenomenon beyond human logic and explanation. As Rumi says:

> "The sign of love is in the misery of heart,
> No sickness is worse than the illness of heart.
> The lover's reasoning is apart from all reasons,
> Love is the astrolabe of God's mysteries."

Why would anybody be crazy to seek love then? The answer is that, love is such a penetrating and gratifying experience nobody can elude its traps. We simply get hypnotized. And once in love, we lose all our willpower, motives, and sleep. We face the mystery of love—the harshest challenge that God has imposed upon humans. So, the question is whether we like to let love affliction make us so helpless we forget even ourselves and our basic needs? Or should we find means of bringing objectivity back into relationships and develop useful guidelines, relationship models, and a framework to help us get a better grasp of life?

Obviously, love defies any sense of logic. The sweetness of love simply knocks one's socks off. We lose ourselves, our minds and consciousness, when we fall in love. Any advice about love or relationships would be the first thing we forget in this circumstance. Yet, a small voice keeps nagging in our heads: "Is it wise to chase love and lose my identity in the process? Should I try to get hold of my emotions somehow?" Sometimes, we eventually succeed to elude love when it cripples our normal routines, reasoning, and behaving. We try to get our sanity back. However, more often than not, as an inevitable consequence of love, its power grabs us by the throat and drags us to the bottom of the pit. By the time we grasp the absurdity of our position, so much of our life and energy is consumed by love—one or many of them. Of course, we seldom feel sorry about any of these inconveniences and losses. The rewards of love, including a mirage of lasting happiness, seem worth all its pains. Yet, eventually, we are somehow forced to renounce love to regain our self. We can live without our 'self' awhile but not indefinitely. We can hold our breath to love someone unconditionally, but we can never stop breathing altogether and not dying. Sometimes, one prefers to die than live without one's beloved. And sometimes, one learns to live selflessly regardless of the response to all his/her passion. Nonetheless, when in love, we become just too ignorant about life and forget how things usually go wrong in relationships that rely on love too much. This is one important truth we can always trust to stay vigilant about our love affairs and relationships.

Another important point is that we seldom have the wisdom and willpower to separate love from relationships. In fact, we normally believe we can turn love into a permanent relationship and we insist on defining relationships mostly by love. Naively we assume that love can guarantee a good relationship. These unrealistic expectations, however, only bring us disappointment. We do not like to separate love from relationships, and even when we do, we have a hard time deciding which one to choose. Each one of these two adventures fulfils a part of our natural needs. However, our eagerness for love usually supersedes our logical pursuit of a relationship. We even leave our not-so-bad relationships for love, or even for the chance of finding love. Like all other myths, love brings us a temporary relief from boredom and life's burdens. It provides a precious remedy for our empty hearts living in such phony societies. Its soothing warmth overrides any kind of logic. We accept the humiliation and agony that comes with it, which could possibly even lead to insanity. We cannot pick a time to love. We have no say about whom we fall in love with and we cannot avoid love traps either. Love just pops out of nowhere accidentally and overwhelms us quickly. On the other hand, we feel the need for a manageable relationship to sustain our routine lives and our sanity. We might come to our senses eventually and abandon our romantic fantasies. This usually happens when love finally fades away or we suffer enough in a few love affairs. Then we start to think of a companion to bring us some peace and stability—the virtues that love usually lacks.

However, relationships, too, are quite difficult to manage nowadays for all the reasons counted in this author's books, which in turn goad us to seek relief in love again, elsewhere, with a different person. The bottom line is that both our love affairs and relationships have become so important, yet agonizing, for reasons of their own. Obviously, there is not much that can be done about the symptoms of love. Often we try to reconcile our needs for both love and a long-term relationship. However, the task of keeping love in relationships is often too difficult. In all, a vicious cycle consumes all the fibres of our existence because of our search for love and a reliable companion.

Ironically, love is a good remedy to forget ourselves and life's hardships, despite (or because of) the agony it eventually imposes upon us. Love is a strong distraction from life's normal hoopla. Even this brief discussion about the mystery love is only for the purpose of bringing some relief to the readers despite all the pessimistic points made throughout this book about the repercussion of allowing love direct our view of relationships.

Understanding the mystery and the joy of love is a good way to bring relief into the purposeless life that everybody must endure. Love is a highly intoxicating feeling that we all enjoy personally, usually with devastating conclusions. Yet, love remains a precious potion and rather manageable as long as one nurtures it solely within him/herself. The anguish begins only when we try to share love with someone else. 'Giving' is a natural symptom of love. We give ourselves, our souls, our wealth, our sanity, and sometimes our integrity to our partners as a price of nourishing love. However, often our partners misunderstand the meaning of our giving. They do not know how to return love with their own authentic feelings and behaviour. On the other hand, a true lover should not care about his/her lover's inability or unwillingness to love him/her back or to behave according to the perfect picture he/she had imagined for his/her beloved. This is the only way to love without getting hurt all the time, which is of course a very difficult proposition for most people.

Despite our shares of disappointments and suffering, we cannot imagine turning away from love if and when it presents itself to us. We all like to remain optimistic about love and perhaps even getting the chance of drawing our last breath with the feeling and thought of a particular love. This is because we know of some exceptions where lovers have been mature enough to sustain their passion for their entire lives. Sometimes, we feel lucky when love embraces us again—God knows for how long. We are glad that he/she has come into our lives. But also think, "God help me!" We just hope that, this time, the new affair would prove to be one of those exceptions where love and tranquility merge within an everlasting relationship.

We may gain new wisdom to make love last a bit longer. The only trick is perhaps to love him/her without expecting too much in return. We may learn to welcome love in its mythical context merely to satisfy our spiritual needs, while set aside all our other expectations from love. How can we avoid the destructive symptoms of love, we wonder? We need immense willpower to do so. Yet we must also prepare ourselves for the high likelihood that a time would arrive when we feel the need to leave our beloved.

At the same time, it is wise to stay alert about the heartbreaking facts of relationships. We must remember the challenge, especially for young couples, to grasp and pursue relationships with open minds away from love. We must learn and remember to assess our partners' personality and incentives for starting or staying in a relationship. It is not easy to generalize the state of relationships so negatively and to stress the obvious fact that a majority of them would fail due to the lack of compassion, logic, trust, or objectivity. Our pessimism can break so many people's (especially women's) delicate hearts, as they see life mainly through love. It is sad that we have so much difficulty nowadays to build our relationships. However, there is not much we can do about this complex situation. It is a sickness that requires a bitter medicine. Just let us hope that we succeed in convincing ourselves to change our mentality about the potentials and purposes of love and relationships, and that social mechanisms are soon revamped drastically too. Adopting such radical solutions to improve the quality of our relationships and reduce personal agonies is difficult, but these changes are absolutely necessary.

Meanwhile, we should enjoy love selflessly, with open eyes and minds about its severe limitations and most likely a sad ending.

The Outlook for Love

Love would always remain a mysterious, thought-provoking topic for humans—the same way life itself has been. Life and love are deeply related, after all. During the last few decades, however, love's ambiguous meaning and exaggerated role in relationships have caused too much complication for people and society. Therefore, the question is, 'How love can survive within the declining atmosphere of modern societies, while we become more reckless every day about our boundless appetite for sexuality?' That is a tough question to study and a tricky outlook to predict. The only positive outcome would perhaps be the wider understanding and use of MLove in relationships in the future as noted below.

In the past, love played a small role in relationships, while poets and philosophers kept people amused with their speculations about it. It had little impact on people's daily lives and their relationships, simply because people did not read many books and were not exposed to such relentless amount of misleading propaganda about love. They had real life hardships to worry about. They were not so obsessed about expressing themselves as much as people in the new era are either. Due to all the new exposures and brainwashing, people have made love the locus of relationships. Love has become confused with attraction and mixed up with many other urges and feelings of humans. The objectives of love and relationships are also muddled up in people's minds. Love and relationships are mostly perceived, even by some scholars, to be synonymous. However, love (SLove) is maybe only 5% of all the urges and activities that go into a relationship. The other urges (sex and compassion) and moods (attraction, romance, and attachment) provide another 45% of the ingredients useful for running a relationship. Thus, the main ingredient of relationships (around 50%) simply relates to its own specific needs and structure, which has been neglected largely in recent decades. We have lost sight of the relationship needs while emphasizing on love (mostly ELove) as the main criterion for starting a relationship and for measuring its health. The rising role of sexuality would continue to have its impact, too, of course. Overall, the destiny of love does not look very bright because:

1. The meaning of love is getting more vague and useless, especially for building relationships. At the same time, we usually like to make a big deal about the phrase "I love you." In effect, the use of the word 'love' has become too hypocritical considering that people have a variety of purposes for, and understanding of, love. Their low capacity for love ruins all their love affairs sooner or later anyway.
2. The general increase in social complexity, sexuality, and corruption makes people less and less trustful of one another and their expressions of love. However, at the same time, people insist that relationships and love must be built on absolute trust and honesty.

Under this circumstance, couples continue to get hurt because of their wrong impressions of love, and because they annoy each other with their exaggerated expectations for love and attention. People destroy not only their chance for building manageable relationships, but also the opportunity of understanding the meaning of SLove. Our limited options to face the reality of love and relationships are:

- To become selfless and internalize SLove, which is a hard task for most of us.
- To pursue love affairs here and there if we are lucky, while the state of our relationships grows more chaotic and instable.
- To live alone while waiting for love (and not knowing how to build relationships).
- To use MLove to instil mutual respect and civility in relationships by overcoming our present craving for ELove and SLove.

The Power of MLove

Using MLove in relationships actually has many advantages. First, it provides a venue for partners to be romantic without raising relationship expectations or creating misunderstandings about their love expressions. Using Mlove makes partners both tactful and proactive for protecting and strengthening their relationships rather naturally. Their mere attempt to remain open and honest about the intention of their love expressions eliminates the need for phoniness and increases the chances of bringing more foreplay into relationships without the fear of creating unsustainable commitments. Within a few decades, the flow of communication between couples would improve, as they eventually learn to apply MLove properly in their relationships. Using a new term, such as MLove, can overcome the cynicism about the phrase 'I love you,' which is losing its value fast.

The next advantage of MLove is that expressing one's feelings through MLove would partially respond to partners' need for SLove. Their deep need for SLove is tentatively satisfied through MLove, which would help them psychologically and physiologically. Although MLove might appear like a kind of role-playing, partners are doing it wholeheartedly in order to simulate SLove. Thus, it is not a forced role-playing, but rather a pleasant, sincere expression of the self.

Another advantage of MLove is that it might also fulfil some of partners' ELove needs. This happens because people's *subconscious* easily substitutes MLove for ELove, while their *conscious* minds remember the purpose of MLove. Therefore, MLove can indirectly satisfy partners' needs for both SLove and ELove, at least partially, while preventing those love expressions from being misinterpreted. In all, partners would not build up too many unwarranted expectations in their relationships simply because they have been expressing nice words (with MLove) to each other. MLove only fills the gap for ELove without increasing partners' expectations from each other, whereas responding to a partner's ELove demands would only feed his/her Ego further and raises his/her need for more ELove.

One important point about MLove is that it is a voluntary and possibly periodical gesture by one or both partners. It could be withdrawn and re-introduced, off and on, in a relationship by one or both partners only at their discretions. Therefore, partners should not turn it into another expectation, otherwise it would be ELove and not MLove anymore.

PART III

Happiness

CHAPTER ELEVEN
'Self' and Happiness

The goal of knowing 'self' (through self-awareness) is twofold: To recognize its essence and keep it content—all in search of that elusive happiness. Without discovering the essence of 'self,' we would never find real happiness, and without a keen desire for true happiness, we would never undertake the horrendous task of knowing our 'self.'

We often believe that a 'formula of happiness' is out there that we may eventually discover to live happily ever after. Despite our rational doubts about the existence of such a formula, after a lifelong of trying and failing to find it, we still keep looking for it because deep down in our hearts we believe that we really *deserve* it. We believe that life is inherently meant to be happy; and that if we do not grasp happiness, it is merely due to our weakness or misfortune. However, our only fault might be our intentional delay or laziness to know our 'self.' We must realize that a relative sense of happiness may emerge only when our means and methods of living satisfy 'self' fully and permanently. Otherwise, there is no evidence that life can be a happy journey. Not everybody deserves happiness, either, especially when we adopt a doomed lifestyle to begin with. In our contaminated social environment, reaching the state of selfhood becomes impossible, since people have rampant superficial needs, materialistic mentality, and low self-awareness. Nonetheless, despite these severe limitations, we still hope that some general ideas about happiness may be drawn from people's life experiences and philosophies.

While we realize that there is no standard formula for happiness, the discussions in Part III are an attempt to establish some general guidelines for finding at least a sense of contentment.

What we may refer to as the formula for happiness is merely a crude account of personal opportunities that might render peace of mind and freedom. Of course, everybody has a unique set of needs and aspirations, which makes a common perception of life or a universal formula for happiness more whimsical. Genetics, family background, and rearing result in personalities that value things differently and make judgments accordingly. Yet, the idea is to examine the possibility of inventing a process or framework that might guide us build a relaxed mindset, regardless of our genetics and perceptions of life. After all, humans' inherent urge to find happiness may not be totally baseless or useless.

Description of Happiness

It feels strange that an ultimate (or common) definition of 'happiness' has not yet been developed and agreed upon in the long history of humanity. All we have after all this time is only sporadic speculations by some philosophers and gurus. A great collection of happiness definitions can be found in *Happiness*, Perennial Books, 2014. Still, finding the right formula, to contain the complex feeling that our wild imagination of happiness suggests, has proven futile so far. We can perhaps describe some of the characteristics and sensations of happiness, as presented in the next section. Yet, even such general descriptions would be incomplete for different types and intensity of happiness that people experience on different occasions and situations.

Overall, 'happiness' merely represents the highs of an emotional roller coaster that our lives ride on. We have learned that happiness is not a steady state, but rather some exotic stances across the dynamic (transient) flow of feelings. We are happy for a short while, before losing our tranquility and looking for it all over again. An absolute and permanent happiness is a myth and fantasy, especially within the rough modes of social living nowadays. A lasting happiness is not psychologically feasible, anyway, due to all kinds of conflicting thought processes and chemical reactions in our brains. Yet, we hopeful humans cannot accept our helplessness to seize happiness as a permanent state and purpose for living. We hate suffering and boredom, so we strive to conquer happiness for good, once and for all. In fact, it does not hurt to imagine that an *absolute* and ultimate happiness is possible under some conditions outside the normal boundaries of human thoughts and wisdom. That is, at some level of wisdom, an ultimate happiness, without ongoing emotional highs and lows, may become plausible. Similar to our impression of the 'afterlife' myth, we can keep ourselves amused with the myth of happiness too.

Misperceptions about Happiness

We look for happiness in many odd places: in our relationships, love affairs, sexuality, spiritual exploration, work, artistic passion, wealth, power, etc. Our job now is to reassess the possibility of finding happiness in any of these endeavours and how. Are any of them causing us only more depression in the end?

Happiness is a myth all by itself, but seeking it in customary means, such as love or relationships, is plain utopian. We have difficulty even defining happiness because it is not a stable state or experience. We only perceive it as an everlasting state of joy and tranquility, which we also expect to result from our endless materialistic desires, greed, and competition. This is a severe contradiction already. We want happiness to fit our contaminated lifestyles, instead of a lifestyle that could induce peace of mind as the closest state of happiness. We forget that any chance for happiness requires a drastic change of personal lifestyle (mainly toward selflessness), which only a few of us might eventually find the courage to effect.

Unfortunately, human nature does not support happiness and tranquility, either, because of innate human urges for challenge, controversy, power, domination, competition, greed, struggle for survival, etc. Anger, hatred, jealousy, spite, and aggressiveness come to us so naturally, but we must try really hard to be honest, compassionate, sincere, and all the other good stuff. Life is not a happy journey either. Our occasional taste of happiness and tranquility soon faces new dilemmas and disappointments. Therefore, as the first step toward tranquility, we must actually learn that happiness is a myth and not a stable state.

In relationships, the notion of happiness becomes even more idealistic because now suddenly two stubborn persons expect each other and their relationship to satisfy their illusory perceptions of happiness, including their egotistical and materialistic needs, pleasure, sexuality, and lasting tranquility. This expectation is actually one major cause of relationship breakdowns. Partners deprive themselves from the basic privileges of relationships because they believe relationships are meant to bring them happiness. They cause themselves more suffering with their obsession for happiness. This is an ironic condition we have brought upon ourselves in recent decades. Instead of learning selflessness and contentment, partners try to strengthen their identities in relationships through arrogance, and then expect happiness too.

Furthermore, most of us mistake pleasures (especially sexuality) with happiness, or assume that more pleasures lead to happiness. So, most relationships become instable soon enough, mostly because they fail to satisfy our fantastic appetite for happiness and sexuality. Of course, we cannot avoid the impression that companionship can fulfil a large number of our personal needs. However, depending on others or relationships to satisfy our personal needs and bring us happiness is naïve and the leading cause of our suffering. Our only chance for tasting this elusive happiness is to seek it within ourselves according to our mental capacity and awareness.

The natural conclusion in most 'happiness' books is that it may be found only inside a person and he/she needs a special mindset to understand and effect this state. This is what this book advocates as well with an emphasis on becoming better humans through personal awareness, to contact our spirit and become needless about many artificial facets of life in the new era. However, this book also stresses on staying practical and grasping our humanistic limitations, which hinder our efforts to be content and a better person.

Some books (quoting philosophers, Buddhism, and the Dalai Lama) suggest that the purpose of life is to find happiness. This notion has been mostly rejected in this book, because life does not have a purpose by itself and humans have many other ambitions besides happiness. The purpose of life (in the context of creation) is neither to spread happiness nor to create good human beings. Happiness is not even the purpose of one's life (regardless of the purpose of the universe). Life is merely a collection of events and moments that transpires in people's lives according to natural laws and chances and affects them based on their cognition (i.e., beliefs, awareness, intelligence, etc.). We all prefer happiness because suffering hurts, and not because it is the purpose of life. We have many higher ambitions in life that we often pursue with greater passion than our desire for happiness or even pleasures, e.g., need for love, power, or recognition. Most of us just cannot sit idle and be happy with our contentment. We resent boredom and we want more adventures even if they cause suffering. We want to be loved even though it often leads to disappointment and pain. The point is that we are not born to be happy or good humans and these are not the purposes of life. We want to become better human beings to soothe our hurts, release tension, or because we sometimes prefer (or like to pretend) to be at peace with ourselves and our surroundings. Happiness and goodness are the probable outcomes of our personal choices to set the right balance between our ambitions and contentment. Life does not have any particular meaning, nor is it about anything in particular. Even if life is about something or has a meaning, God has not yet revealed it to us through His prophets, nor has He given us enough intelligence to figure it out.

The slogan 'life is for the purpose of happiness' is in fact causing more suffering than guiding people toward happiness. The reason is that it makes people believe that such a myth (happiness) actually exists, and that the reason they cannot find it is due to their stupidity or relationships. They feel incompetent and frustrated. They leave their relationships prematurely or seek all kinds of pleasures and sexuality to attain the purpose of life, i.e., happiness. But then they feel even more empty and lost.

Most importantly, life is not for the purpose of getting hung up over a mythical concept like happiness and causing extra suffering for ourselves. Ninety-nine percent of us cannot find that elusive happiness. The one percent who claims to have found it, like monks and priests, must make many sacrifices, limit their social activities, and accept celibacy and suffering in order to maintain their state of contentment, which they call happiness. It seems that happiness has a lot to do with selflessness, meditation, celibacy, and absorbing sufferings. However, by nature, most of us are selfish, and like our sexuality and pleasures a lot, which would accordingly lead to unhappiness. How many of us are willing to be celibate, limit our pleasures and social lives, and welcome sufferings to reach the height of enlightenment (for happiness)? We must really force ourselves to fulfil most of these requirements, which shows happiness can never be a natural pursuit of humans, especially in our materialistic world. Accordingly, the purpose of our existence is not to seek happiness, as the Dalai Lama says, because we humans are not prepared to pay the price for it and we are not made for it. We must think and act within our natural capacities, while aiming to be better human beings too. In particular, blaming our relationships and partners for not inducing the happiness that we cannot find anywhere else on our own is a silly attitude prevalent in society nowadays.

The fact that we crave happiness in vain reveals our inner turmoil and inability to define our existence in simpler terms personally.

Characteristics of a 'Happiness' Experience

To describe happiness, we should explore, i) What happiness is—the 'feeling,' ii) What generates it—the 'cause,' iii) What it does to us—the 'impact,' and iv) What we do with it—the 'effect.'

The Feeling: The ultimate happiness is a deep inner feeling of joy, relief, tranquillity, self-satisfaction, self-fulfilment, lightness, transcendence, completeness, mental pleasure, freedom, needlessness, independence, mental strength, love, and a sense of mind-body interaction. Our happiness experiences may not be as complete as described by all these feelings, but rather entail a good bunch of them in good proportions. Yet, a complete happiness potentially contains all the above ingredients and more, in large proportions. Overall, happiness is the sign and sentiment of a freed spirit.

The Cause: Happiness manifests in different ways as a result of an achievement or discovery, a new joyful experience, after some physical pleasure, at the end of a depression cycle, upon removal of a burden, through passion, sudden hopefulness about something, recognition and psychological fulfilment, compassion and support, spirituality, etc.

The Impact: Happiness brings us a high level of energy and rejuvenation, courage, humanness, and we become more forgiving and tolerant of others. We feel our spirits lifted and our outlook on life improved drastically.

The effect: In general, when we are happy, we enjoy life much more and maintain our physical and psychological health better and longer. We are compassionate and affect the life of others more positively by bouncing off rays of hope, joy, and humour. A truly happy person has a high level of energy, creativity, and humanness, and transmits his compassion and joy to others through positive attitude and taking on more activities and responsibilities.

A true happiness experience contains all these four elements (characteristics) in full. That is, happiness is not only a 'feeling,' and a feeling of happiness is not an end in itself. The 'cause' of happiness determines the depth and longevity of the feeling. And the feeling itself initiates a chain of internal and external reactions that impact the person's health and attitude and consequently affect other events, things, and people around him. Our happiness experiences often seem incomplete and short-lived because one or more of its four elements are missing or weak. Possibly the 'cause' has not been strong or legitimate. Or the 'feeling' has not been deep and deserved. Or the experience has no lasting 'impact' on us. And perhaps the 'effect' of our happiness is not adequately transmitted to other venues or people. These types of presumed happiness experiences, or tentative pleasures, are nice to have, but they are not deep and effective enough to consider a real happiness experience. For example, when we hear a joke, have casual sex, or find out that someone we hate is hurt, we feel happy for only a short period. On the other hand, a real happiness evolves only upon the completion of a full cycle of cause, feeling, impact, and effect. The stronger, more authentic, and fuller the cycle of the four elements, the longer and more effective the experience would be.

Along with the completeness of the four characteristics (elements) of happiness, the frequency of happiness experiences is obviously important, too. Generally, the feeling of happiness fades away when the 'impact' and the 'effect' are no longer present. When we forget the impact of our happiness, maybe because the 'cause' of it has not been strong enough, and when we lose our energy to 'affect' others or things, the whole cycle stops and happiness ends. Therefore, we need the continuity of the cycle—the cause, the feeling, the impact, and the effect. A 'formula' of happiness can merely refer to the necessity of keeping this cycle active and vibrant. Only the high frequency and speed of the cycle may guarantee a longer-lasting happiness. Self-awareness is required to feed the cycle properly and permanently in order to prevent it from leakage and exhaustion.

The causes of happiness by themselves consist of those experiences and events that happen to a person accidentally, and those that he specially plans for. For example, winning a lottery is a less effective 'cause' for happiness compared to a personal achievement resulting from diligent planning and efforts. The first kind of 'cause,' which is merely a fluke, leads only to a short-term happiness, because in essence, the cause is often not strong and genuine enough and usually not driven by authentic personal urges. Of course, a lottery windfall makes the winner ecstatic for a short while. However, it is not a legitimate cause of happiness because the person has played no effective role in achieving the rewards. The impact of happiness would wear off quickly too, since the same winning experience hardly happens again. Even if it kept happening every week, its impact would vanish after a couple of weeks. Thus, the person must find other causes to stir the sense of happiness in him. He may be able to use his fortune wisely to stir opportunities that cause full cycles of happiness, but the new causes would be the real sources of feeding the cycle, not the initial cause, i.e., winning a lottery.

Overall, the initial efforts and intentions of the individual are crucial for creating a fulfilling and meaningful 'cause' of happiness. Besides, since the 'cause' of happiness is under his control, he can extend his efforts more consciously to recreate the outcomes that would repeat the same experiences of happiness. In effect, by doing the right kind of stuff on an ongoing basis, the person contributes directly and continuously to the recreation of happiness experiences. Thus, the old saying that, 'We create our own happiness,' with our intentional involvement and awareness of the process, especially controlling the 'cause' of happiness. The potency of the 'cause' determines the depth of the other three elements of happiness, i.e., feeling, impact, and effect.

With this basic description of happiness elements in place, the next step is to explore how happiness materializes for people, and whether and how the depth of their happiness may relate to individual's personality. Correlating people's personality aspects (Model, Ego, Self) with happiness elements (i.e., feeling, cause, impact, and effect) helps us understand the myth of happiness better. We find that most happiness experiences are not genuine, deep, and effective because the four happiness elements react differently according to the personality aspects of individuals experiencing them.

The Happiness of 'Model'

Model is the practical face of a person attempting to hide his gullibility, neediness, fears, selfishness, Ego, and his psychological defects from others. Model satisfies most of our *social and belongingness needs* by trying to adapt to the rules of society and becoming part of it. It is the aspect that justifies our *actions and decisions* within ordained social norms, which Model is expected to know and conform to. It speaks and acts to impress others and obtain the psychological support we crave so desperately. Therefore, the more Model emphasizes on satisfying our shallow needs for approval, belongingness, and social status, the more our higher needs, including self-esteem and self-realization, remain neglected.

Ordinarily, moving up the 'personal needs tree' boosts the cycles of happiness, as long as the individual is aiming for the opportunity of satisfying his self-actualization and spirituality needs. So, finding real happiness becomes impossible when an individual stops at a low level and keeps striving for the same lower need satisfaction repeatedly. Remaining stagnant at a low level is against Maslow's theory that presumes people understand, plan, and strive for their higher-level needs intuitively. Stagnation is against humans' basic instincts. In reality, however, it happens quite often as people do not know or care about their higher-level needs—mostly because their Model and medium-range needs keep them on a substandard path of life. Even if Model was not so dominant and we appreciated the ultimate needs of our being, we do not find time, or know how, to aim for satisfying our higher needs, e.g., spirituality.

Persisting at lower personal (psychological) needs, e.g., for love or social status, actually results in frustration since no amount of love and social status seems sufficient; and a small breakdown in their supply feels disastrous. Like some kind of addiction, our tentative happiness comes from satisfying our mental or physical dependency. Attached to this urgent and short-lived need satisfaction are anxiety and self-pity, as this habit creates only more craving and dependency on others.

The 'cause' of happiness for Model stems from other people's recognition of his work or attitude. Thus, even his tentative sense of happiness breaks repeatedly while he remains at the mercy of others. It is impossible for people to understand an individual and give him enough credit for who he really is, let alone who he is pretending to be as a Model. In fact, people would see the superficiality of the Model eventually and the approval pipeline starts leaking again. Thus, he now must strive to find a new group of people to confirm his existence. This mental conundrum is never fixed until the person stops the pattern of feeding his addiction and begins moving up the ladder of the needs tree to gain some sense of independence.

We could be rude and consider a 'model' dominated personality a phony character with no originality and authenticity. We could even take him as a charlatan or hypocrite trying to manipulate others by pretending to be caring or compassionate. However, at best, he is a simpleton eluding his real identity in hopes of impressing others or hiding his idiosyncrasies. He strives to manage a secondary personality, which only reflects his apprehension about his primary personality or inability to build one. These inner conflicts for Model prevent the development of a legitimate 'cause' for happiness.

Sometimes, Model adopts a personality stronger and healthier than his primary (flawed) personality for improving himself. This is an honourable exercise and a great achievement if he succeeds internalizing some of the Self's traits through the Model he has adopted. This high achievement would provide a legitimate 'cause' of happiness for him. In such exceptional instances, the Model might help a person proceed toward independence and a 'self' dominated personality through self-awareness.

While some moderate Model is useful for social adaptation, etiquette, and coping, Model domination shows either a person's deep neediness or his immaturity and insecurities. A Model driven by immaturity imitates a personality with needs that are neither in line with his own nor authentic per se. He simply pursues some inferior needs just for playing the role of a particular model, e.g., as a gang member.

The 'impact' of Model's performance and achievements would be at best a tenuous happiness and thus not heartfelt. Often, his conscience turns against the Model and perhaps induces an internal resentment and competition with this fake personality. We may recall those instances where we did not feel so proud deep down in our hearts when in fact our Model was quite satisfied with the performance and outcome. For example, as part of the initiation in a fraternity or sorority, we may engage in activities that are normally not quite a part of our real character. We do things to get the acceptance of others. Afterward, we feel down and confused as our conscience asks why? Role-playing a Model, we tell our kids not to lie, but then do exactly the same thing ourselves, sometimes even in front of them.

A Model feels excited and happy when he makes up stories about his wisdom or courage to get the respect of his family and others. However, the Self, observing the masquerade from inside, knows how cowardly he has twisted the facts to serve his Ego. Happiness of the Model is thus shaky because the person knows that he is only serving his Ego with no Self respect or satisfaction.

The success in selling 'who one pretends to be' presumably constitute a Model's cause of happiness. If the outcome is effective enough and repeatable, it would only encourage the person to pursue the needs of the Model and depress his own (ones that are more natural) even further. The 'cause' of happiness is weak, anyway, but still those repeated tentative happy instances encourage the person to reinforce the 'model' personality and thus accelerate the destruction of his real personality, or jeopardizes the possibility of growing a more authentic and independent character.

The tentative rewards that Model receives for adaptation and approval do not serve him in the long run anyway. A Model is always running the risk of being exposed to others sooner or later, often when he becomes most popular and attached to the incentives and causes of his happiness, which he is now quite addicted to and counting on. During this process, he continues to quarrel within himself—with his deprived real nature, which he is personally trying so hard to suppress. Like any actor that often loses his own identity by playing the role of a character continuously, a Model gets confused about who he really is. The more a person is successful as a 'model' personality, the faster he is detached and alienated from his inner needs and instincts. He often learns to like what he is, or is doing, as a Model, while he would increasingly feel anxious without knowing why.

A Model often transforms into a happy-go-lucky person, due to the effect of positive thinking propagandas and the social appeal to always portray a positive attitude. Yet, deep down, he often feels unhappy, frustrated, unfulfilled, and tired of playing games all the time. Constant doubting of one's identity subconsciously does not bring a healthy lifestyle for anybody. However, it is even worse for a Model, because his disguise becomes superficial and ineffective faster if he cannot portray the positive reflection of a truly happy person constantly regardless of how he really feels. Sometimes, we are bound to keep a happy face to pretend we like our jobs, are happy with our relationships, to appear tactful and respectful, etc. Perhaps there is not much harm in keeping a happy face as a gesture of mannerism and social behaviour to the extent that we do not get absorbed into this superficiality deeply. As another exception noted before, using Model to reinforce our inner needs and reach selfhood (and perhaps a natural sense of optimism) is an honourable and productive process.

Sometimes, a person keeps switching from one Model to a different Model, hoping to find his real niche. He usually switches when he does not get what he had expected from a Model or because he becomes frustrated after playing the role of that Model for a while. When a person fails to play a role properly, or when people detect his shallow personality, he must find a new mask. The mental health of the person switching from Model to Model suffers even more than the case of a person who has a more stable role to play, even as a Model. There would be no deep 'cause' of happiness in a cycle like this, as the person becomes highly confused about his identity and mission in life when he switches the role model and disappointments mount with every switch. A simple version of this situation is when a person cannot decide on a career and switches between jobs and every time finds a reason to quit. He cannot figure out his real vocational needs (and potentialities).

The 'cause' of happiness, e.g., getting approval and acceptance, not only undermines his authentic needs toward self-fulfilment, but also encourages him to become more phony and shallow every day. His time and energy are wasted on goals ineffective for his psychological growth or improving his idiosyncrasies. Of course, the underlying reason for being a Model is his insecurity and immaturity in the first place. Thus, he is unaware or careless about his other personal needs beyond the needs of the Model anyway. In fact, his urge to repeat the same experience to stay happy only reinforces his conscious or subconscious efforts to suppress his instincts even deeper and run away from his real needs faster. Accordingly, Model is less likely to ask 'who am

I?', because he keeps justifying to himself why he likes to be somebody else.

In all, for a Model, the 'cause' of happiness is something or somebody, which he generally has no, or very little, control over. When the 'cause' of happiness remains so shaky and irrelevant for Model, the other elements of happiness, i.e., the 'feeling', 'impact', or 'effect,' always remain too tentative too.

The 'feeling' of happiness is shallow and usually offset by the constant, subconscious fear of losing the momentum when the effect of his pretensions wears off. The happiness cannot make a major 'impact' on him since the presumed rewards are irrelevant for realizing his higher psychological needs. And obviously, a Model cannot 'affect' others (especially people with low Model orientation) positively as he cannot connect to anybody truthfully. Even when he does something for someone, it would be insincere and only out of fear of losing that person's approval, or for satisfying a selfish purpose, e.g., manipulating someone, or he is simply trying to conform to some rules just to maintain his status, e.g., his job. And, of course, the cycle of happiness itself is often impaired quickly in the case of a Model, when the approval and acceptance channels dry up even temporarily.

It is interesting, and sad, how our social values and environments encourage a Model attitude (compliance and hypocrisy) in particular. And it is even more interesting how, in fact, Model personalities help satisfy the dependency needs of one another by promoting phony social values and norms, despite their knowledge of the low sincerity and integrity of the words they exchange. By giving and receiving compliments, Models support one another's psychological needs for external approval and social status. Like an addiction, a Model craves attention although he knows it is phony and perhaps even a means of being exploited. Salespeople know this weakness of Models (in the general public) and use it to the extreme. Models usually say things differently in the presence and absence of a person, which often is a sign of both their hypocrisy and desperation. Unfortunately, 'model' oriented personalities are increasing in society and they are pushing phonier social values and behaviour too. Therefore, we find more depression in society than real happiness.

The Happiness of 'Ego'

Ego handles our value systems, judgments and punishments, senses of competition and superiority, desires and expectations. It reflects the *real intentions* of our words and actions, and our *re-actions* to other people's words and actions. An egoist is self-centred with extreme expectations and narrow perceptions of others, and he is harsh in his judgments and punishments with a dramatically biased value system. Ego is an exact opposite to Model in many ways, especially frankness, impatience, and pomposity. Therefore, a person's Model and Ego often clash and cause extra headaches for him. However, they also help each other, e.g., when Ego uses Model as a strategy to manipulate another person.

Unlike Model, an egoist's needs often extend across all levels of the personal needs tree. In particular, he is too ambitious with a high need for achievement and recognition. He has an extreme need for control and doing things his way. Yet, his achievements remain non-actualizing because his self-serving objectives usually supersede the sense of purity and selflessness that self-actualization requires. Therefore, while an egoist may have many experiences of achievement and thrill, they are seldom actualizing and they hardly cause lasting happiness.

An egoist attempts to use a scheme or his charm (through Model) for attracting and exploiting others. However, an egoist does not have the patience and motivation of a Model to attract people merely for the sake of friendship. If his hidden intentions are not satisfied quickly through pretensions of Model, he gets frustrated and resorts to a different strategy, e.g., aggression, to satisfy his important and urgent need for self-gratification.

The Ego's 'cause' of happiness relates to the outcome of his selfish actions and intentions. He works hard to serve his Ego for the highest level of thrill and satisfaction. He must keep boosting his Ego to feel happy, mostly by getting things done in the *manner* he desires, which is often more important than the outcome itself. He can forget his failures and forgive himself quickly as long as he succeeds in making everybody follow his lead. He is convinced that his judgments are always fair, logical, and appropriate. When he seems to compromise, he is simply using Model for manipulation and exploitations.

An egoist is stubborn and certain about all the *facts* in the world. He believes he knows everything and has the answers for all the problems, while others are ignorant and inferior to him in logic and vision. His high expectations from others and himself usually remain unfulfilled because his goals are unrealistic, his expectations from others are more selfish than rational, his directions are too rigid, and also because individuals' Egos clash all the time. Simply due to his demanding personality, seldom an egoist gets satisfied with either the outcomes or the means of achieving them.

Egoists' inflated Ego and inherent drive for gratification push them to take risk and set tough (and often unrealistic) objectives. However, their needs for control and self-importance stop them from putting their guards down to find their Self. They have wrong perceptions about the means of satisfying their needs, especially the higher ones for which a true self-actualizer must depend merely on himself instead of exploiting others to get things done.

An egoist's 'cause' of happiness also relates to other people's reactions to his expectations. Often his happiness is at the expense of those whom he exploits. It depends on someone else's submission and willingness to play along with his game of exploitation and manipulation. Naturally, in most cases this expectation cannot last long and causes many frictions.

An egoist's 'feeling' of happiness comes from shallow short-lived gratifications, because his objectives are self-serving and often achieved by pushing others. Therefore, he must keep manipulating others and struggle for more signs and symbols of achievements to boost his Ego and maintain his shaky cycles of happiness. The more he depends on people to achieve certain goals, the more he must feed this cycle (by pushing others) to maintain the momentum. Even his tentative satisfaction from his achievements merely boosts his Ego rather than soothing his soul. He is *ruled* by his Ego and lives to satisfy it—a never-ending struggle to preserve his pompous identity.

His shallow feelings of happiness cannot 'impact' him, as he has no time or patience to stop and contemplate on his fulfilments and their true meanings. He often does not even know, or care about, the real purposes of his struggles while he follows certain routines aggressively. Artificial objectives, such as maximizing wealth and power, justify all his struggles. His triumphs have no relationship to his essential and inherent needs. And of course, when he is unaware of the relationship between his real needs and triumphs, he can never internalize his achievements. Thus, the rewards and fulfilments cannot impact him deeply. The only 'impact' of his fulfilments is his eagerness to repeat his mischievous and exploitative activities that boost his Ego and give him some wicked feelings of satisfaction.

Accordingly, he has no ability to affect others either, except for the burden of his manipulative attitude that intimidate others. Thus, for an egoist whose fulfilments come at the expense of hurting others, the 'effect' of his accomplishments is negative. Egoists' plans and actions are always calculating and self-serving for specific personal interests, either for an immediate benefit or future exploitation. Doing things for the sake of 'affecting' others positively does not mean anything to an egoist unless it has some advantage for him personally, and this scenario seldom happens.

The cycle of happiness for an 'egoist' is too short and thus s/he requires extreme momentum to maintain even a tentative sense of happiness. Otherwise, frustration and stress take over quickly. A tremendous level of effort is required to feed the cycle and still real happiness is hard to maintain.

Establishing a working relationship with others is extremely difficult for an egoist even when s/he tries to use his/her Model. Particularly, establishing a mutually acceptable marital relationship and teamwork atmosphere would be very difficult for egoists. These kinds of attitudes are, unfortunately, prevalent and somehow even encouraged in our societies as a means of establishing partners' individuality. They lead to constant psychological struggles that hinder partners' communication and happiness. Work environments are becoming quite difficult to tolerate, too, due to the rising number of egoists and psychopaths running organizations nowadays. The negative effects of these people's managerial style have brought the level of social stress to a record high.

The Happiness of 'Self'

Self holds our basic instincts, feelings, and needs, including spirituality. It holds our potentialities, genius, creativity, and psychic energy. This aspect of our personality also contains our innocence, conscience, and regrets. Self is our *real being* outside the conditioning rules of society, aside from the value systems that we have decided to adopt and adapt ourselves to. Perhaps a symbolic representation of Self can be found in Tarzan whose instincts and feelings are intact and pure. However, Tarzan is merely a raw picture of Self, while his potentialities and spirituality dimensions remain untapped.

We all meditate in some form, either consciously or subconsciously, to get close to our Self, although we often know very little about the meaning of Self or the means of reaching that pure state of being. When we go to a church, mosque, or shrine to speak to our Gods, we are doing some form of meditation to contact our Self—our soul. We need to do this meditation, at least in private, in order to heal our physical and psychological hurts from living. We need to go somewhere in Nature alone and think, quiet our minds and understand what our inner voices are saying. These are the basic experiences of Self that most of us have enjoyed at least a few times. However, on most occasions, we do not recognize and appreciate them as a device for entering our most intimate, yet neglected, state of natural being and for finding some relative freedom at least. We bypass the opportunity to delve into our Selfhood after a short pause at the entrance every time we meditate.

Contrary to the situations for Model and Ego that require external stimuli for approaching some form of happiness, the happiness of Self is automatic. The only requirement is to acknowledge the Self that is within every one of us ready to be explored and nurtured. It is surely not a straightforward and easy task, but it is possible to get at least a little acquainted with Self. The first step is to believe in the possibility of being a better human being for our own sake at least and then learn how. Afterward, we can use the power of Self to overcome the negative influences of Model and Ego at any opportunity. Every time we let Self overcome the Ego's or Model's attempt to taint our deeds and decisions, we get one step closer to realizing Self. It cannot happen overnight, but with practice and active meditation, we can give our Self the power to overrule Model and Ego when they try to dominate our existence and behaviour.

How is the happiness of Self automatic? And how the elements of happiness, i.e., cause, feeling, impact, and effect apply to Self?

The 'causes' of happiness for Self are several. The main cause, which is perhaps less tangible to people with no or little experience of Self, comes from the achievement of being a Self dominated personality per se. We can imagine how a caged animal feels once it escapes. We know how much risk and trouble prisoners are willing to endure to find a way to flee. Reaching Self dominance resembles these experiences of freedom, except that finding Self would be even a more meaningful and permanent experience. Once a person learns to recognize and free his Self from the captivity of Model and Ego, he enters the world of eternal peace and tranquillity in which happiness is automatic. There is no need to feed a cycle of happiness in order to maintain it, as long as one stays in the kingdom of Selfdom. The happiness of Self is inherent. Merely our superficial needs and the influence of Ego and Model suffocate this natural source of happiness.

There is no need to discuss the other 'causes' of happiness of Self when the main cause is so prominently adequate. Yet, some other elements of happiness for a Self-driven person are interesting to discuss.

A Self dominated person finds the opportunity and strength to realize humans' essential (but hidden) potentialities. By saving the energies normally wasted by Model and Ego, Self focuses on the means of actualizing himself. He concentrates on thoughts and activities that nurture the real nature of a person rather than the ones that hurt and destroy his physical and mental abilities. Generating valuable ideas, exploring the creative domains of mind, and maintaining the vision of a universal existence, provide happiness experiences that replace, or at least mitigate, the mundane tasks of living and surviving. The purpose of one's being becomes vivid and meaningful. Simple thoughts and activities derived from the energies of the inner 'self' turn into self-actualizing and spiritual experiences. Oneness with the universe that rules our being manifests as unique moments of ecstasy and experiences beyond the meanings of the worldly pleasures. These are some other 'causes' of happiness of Self.

A 'self' dominated person does not depend on outside world to induce a 'cause' of happiness. He finds the sources of fulfilment without exploiting others and expecting approvals from other people. He is not threatened by the punishments of the power-thirsty authorities of our world, nor does he care about the luring rewards of compliance. He is neither attached to the worldly values that control him, nor detached of the harmonic worldly relationships that complement his being and co-existence. The challenge for maintaining this delicate balance constitutes some other 'causes' of happiness for Self.

All these 'causes' of happiness are Self directed and not controllable by outsiders. Therefore, the happiness generated through these experiences is manageable much better by the individual and remain more consistent and repeatable by him. He is in control of the 'causes.'

The 'feelings' of happiness, which are induced by self-controlled 'causes,' prolongs rather continuously, and they are authentic and deep, with a lasting impact. There are hardly any interruptions in the 'causes and feeling.' In fact, for a Self-driven personality, the 'feelings' and 'causes' are usually the same thing, because the cause of happiness is inherent for Self, as noted earlier. This natural property gives the whole cycle of happiness more momentum, intensity, and continuity. Maslow's descriptions of self-actualizers' feelings provide great evidence of how deep those sensations are, and how they directly relate to, and connect with, the causes.

The 'impacts' of Self-controlled happiness are fundamental and coincide with the 'cause-feeling' interconnectivity. The impacts are psychological, spiritual, and a source of tranquillity.

The 'effects' are also paramount and continuous. A 'self' dominated person has a different view of people, events and things. In particular, he has a great deal of compassion toward everybody despite his profound knowledge of people's inherent impurity and frequent malice. He feels connected to the whole universe and knows that he is an inseparable part of it, including all the badness within and outside him. Therefore, everything he does is automatically and directly affecting other things and people in a positive way, simply because they reinforce his own 'cause' of happiness. To him, the give and take are the same things and have the same meaning and effect. In all, the four elements of happiness have an integrated and integral interconnectivity that drive a cycle of permanent and self-nurturing happiness experiences. This cycle accelerates even faster once one's ability of utilizing the potentials of Self are largely developed.

Personality Aspects' Role for Happiness

The above discussions of the three aspects of personality suggest that happiness can happen only to Self. The happiness of the other personality aspects is at best shallow and temporary. Usually one or two of a person's three aspects of personality overwhelm the other(s). We may remember many evidences supporting the dominance of a particular personality aspect over others during our interactions and relationships. Overall, however, we usually do not detect enough of our own Model or Ego the same way we notice them so quickly in other people. This low awareness about ourselves is in line with our general tendency to miss our psychological defects unless we make a point of exploring them. We simply deny our Model and Ego despite the comments and clues we receive from others as well as our own conscience.

We do not believe or admit that we are anything but a pure Self. We do not like to admit that our prominent Model prevents us from understanding who we are and what our purpose of living is. We would never accept the idea of our strong Ego depriving us from sensing compassion and having a tranquil and happy life. Obviously, we would not find the courage and incentive to study our Self until we acknowledge these sad facts. Unless we admit that we have become slaves to Model and Ego, we would never believe in any of the suggestions about Self and happiness.

We hate to admit that our weaknesses and lack of happiness in life are the result of letting Model and Ego run our lives. Even if we get the courage to admit it to ourselves, we have a hard time taming these crooked aspects within us. How would a Model or Ego consider adopting a more 'self' controlled personality? Initially, he would not even have an idea what being a Self means, how it works, what it requires, etc. However, realistically, if he is going to give up, or at least tame, his Model or Ego, he would first require a tangible understanding of Self and the way he should act and behave from within this aspect of his personality. He is estranged to Self, and actually, his Self has never had a chance to grow. Without a relatively comprehensive grasp of Self, the switch would be impossible regardless of our efforts. Playing Self (e.g., as a Good Samaritan) without understanding its meaning is merely another attempt for building a different Model personality. To remain realistic, the switch to selfhood must be gradual and in line with one's appreciation and practice of a Self-controlled life.

This book talks about 'self' in different dimensions and from different angles. We try in different ways to explain what 'self' really means, how we can find it in ourselves, and how we need to use its potentialities to make our lives tolerable and perhaps happy. Still at the end, what this book can offer is only a general idea of what 'self' really is. Everybody must explore it individually and maybe find a personal interpretation of 'self' in terms of definition and application, though the same source of energy manifests and directs us through life. Therefore, an ultimate definition of 'self,' or how exactly it leads to happiness is somewhat personal. Just by trying to become a better human being would get us there. Detecting and defusing our Ego and Model bring out the Self automatically.

The degree and depth of our happiness depend on the varying prominence of Model, Ego, and Self at any time, and thus our happiness experiences find different qualities and properties. We have *a kind of* multiple personalities due to an aspect of our personality becoming more dominant in various instants. This also indicates that expecting a continuous happiness mood is almost impossible even for a Self dominated person. Although a Self-controlled personality has the highest chance of carrying a tranquil and happy life, still the other two aspects of his personality emerge occasionally in small doses. When Model or Ego takes over temporarily, even a 'self' dominated person thinks and behaves erratically. The firmer his Self-control, the less frequent

Model or Ego finds a chance to interfere. Nonetheless, the random dominance of Model or Ego is normal. We should expect moments of distress even when we have a genuine Self dominated personality. There are several reasons for these moments of weakness erupting.

First, our temporary switch to Model or Ego, as a requirement of coping and living, might cause experiences that ruin all our previous triumphs and thus lead to a cycle of depression. For example, we might submit to adultery or some other mischief in a moment of weakness. This experience brings a sense of discomfort and delusion that overrides an enduring cycle of happiness. Our conscience might bother us for a long time.

Second, it is possible that occasionally we neglect to attend to our Self. Although the happiness cycle for Self is automatic and self-nurturing, remaining a 'self' dominated person demands constant *awareness*. If we forget our need for ongoing meditation and development of Self, the 'self'-control process stops, Model and Ego take over, and the happiness cycle breaks.

Third, even for a 'self' dominated person, moments of doubts and questioning erupt, especially when it becomes necessary to adapt himself to social demands and get along with people. During those moments of self-doubt we question our choices and paths, we think about our sanity and philosophy of life, we think about our responsibilities and financial obligations, we suffer from our solitude and loneliness, we think about our relationships that we are hoping to 'self'-control, etc. Under these circumstances, we are psychologically vulnerable and undergo a state of mild depression, if not something more serious.

Nevertheless, some inconsistencies in the level of our happiness should be expected, even for a 'self' dominated person. Developing 'self'-control becomes important for managing these irregularities in our lives, too. The more we grasp and practise a 'self' dominated life, the better we can cope with, and defeat, the periods of temporary distress or doubts.

CHAPTER TWELVE
Personality and Depression

Our awareness about the role of personality aspects in creating happiness cycles and experiences is only half of our challenge. The other half pertains to our ability to endure and defeat the cycles of depression. Happiness and depression are contending forces that clash in our psyches all the time. Therefore, our search for happiness is futile when some sneaky forces of depression bombard us. They are either generated internally from within us, often unconsciously, or imposed upon us by outside sources. We should understand the nature of these two sources of depressions and mitigate their impacts. However, our personality is responsible for creating most of our depression and suffering. While Self is conduit for finding happiness, personality causes depression.

Thus, depression should also be measured in reference to the three aspects of personality, i.e., Model, Ego, and Self even more closely than 'happiness' was dissected in the previous chapter. In particular, every aspect of personality plays a different role in creating self-induced depressions. They also have different strengths for fighting the forces of depressions from outside sources, such as social, financial, and relationships. Furthermore, the same elements of happiness, i.e., cause, feeling, impact, and effect, apply equally to depression. Therefore, we can evaluate the forces of depression from within the same framework, i.e., by gauging the effect of each aspect of personality on the four elements of depression.

We should actually study two issues about our depression according to the three aspects of the personality: First, we must find out how each of these personality aspects generates self-induced depression. Second, we must study how a person dominated with any one of these personality aspects deals with depressions caused by inner or outer sources, (i.e., coming from within or outside him.)

The Depression of 'Model'

The self-induced depression of Model accumulates inherently from his inability to move up the 'personal needs tree' and fulfil his higher needs, including spirituality. He is not quite aware of those needs and that his neglect to satisfy them hinders his psychological growth and self-image. Yet the lack of fulfilment creates boredom, which is obviously a hidden source of depression for everybody. Not knowing the real sources of his boredom, about his higher needs, and how to attend to them, are the 'causes' of his depression. Furthermore, his needs for approval, love, and sense of belonging cause him stress and self-pity when they do not happen enough in reality or he doubts their authenticity. He gets disappointed with himself and others, so he continues to develop new tactics to get the love and approval he needs so desperately. He tries to play his role as a Model more precisely and effectively and thus becomes phonier. He exhausts himself by wasting all his energy seeking attention and recognition instead of dealing with his authentic inner needs. All these strenuous efforts and reactions are hidden causes of self-induced depression.

The depth of depression is the highest for Model, as he feels too helpless without a large dose of external attention on a regular basis. His only sense of psychological security in life is given to him by outsiders. He must try hard to maintain this safety net.

Therefore, he ignores his other psychological urges in order to concentrate on these low-level needs. This incessant struggle (strategies and activities) for acceptance and love by itself reinforces the cycles of depression vigorously and frequently and makes the task of self-redemption too difficult.

With respect to 'externally induced' depressions, Model is quite vulnerable, because he is always extremely anxious to cope with external forces and fit within society rather like an obsession. The 'causes' of his depression relate to any of social, financial, political, or relationship problem that he seems unable to solve. When there is a problem in one or more of these areas, it means that there is a conflict between a Model's *urgent* expectations and what he actually gets. This conflict to Model usually means rejection or his inability to adapt. He takes the matter too personal, due to low self-image and high oversensitivity. He feels defeated, misunderstood, and ignored, especially considering all his efforts to be loved and understood. Somebody or some mechanism is not taking his efforts or his needs seriously. It does not matter how in practice he deals with these external sources of his depression. He may take a legal action, retaliate against his companion or spouse, try to become more accommodating, leave the company he is working for, etc. The important point is that internally he has to deal with the pressures of coping and possible rejections, which he has a hard time accepting as a reality of life. His high expectations for being always understood and accepted hardly match reality, while he also naively over-trusts human nature. Thus, he faces a major dilemma often when people's reactions seem odd and unfair to him/her. A rejection, in whatever form, is extremely personal and unbearable for him emotionally, even more than it may hurt his Ego, and thus results in a deep depression. As expected, Model is mentally prepared to hide the setbacks and his emotions, instead of confronting his opponents assertively. Actually, Model develops a strong defence mechanism to take rejections lightly in the surface and jump to other opportunities to satisfy his need for acceptance and approval. Yet, every rejection brings him deep depression, plus the added pressures of hiding his frustration. Thus, he suffers for it internally longer than if he somehow dealt with his depression and people's aggression more assertively or just ignored it rather stoically.

The cause, feeling, impact, and effect of depression for both types of self-induced and imposed depressions follow the same pattern. The 'causes' of his depression are numerous as delineated throughout this section. The 'feelings' of depression are quite deep and devastating for Model, although he attempts to appear calm and collected for playing his role (as part of Model).

The 'impact' and 'effect' of such depression are obviously harsh and harmful to him and other people around him. It is very likely that his oversensitivity and repeated rejections (two other causes of his depression by themselves) lead to low self-image, self-loathing, and passive aggression, which he would also try to hide and control as much as possible. Signs of his neediness for affection and attention also show in his sudden, occasional outburst or even his pretentious show of compassion. The irony is that, with spreading negative 'effects' on others, as a result of his neediness and smothered depression, he annoys the same people he depends on for love. He turns gradually into an oversensitive person who expects unconditional attention and love, but is often incapable of providing true compassion to others despite his pretensions. People usually have a hard time dealing with these ultra sensitive individuals and odd (uncomfortable) situations that emerge from such interactions. In general, everybody has difficulty finding the right level of Model to adapt and get adequate approval without becoming too needy and rejected.

The Depression of 'Ego'

The self-induced depression of Ego is caused by his inability to achieve enough of his goals and expectations, in terms of not only results, but also the *means* of attaining them. He becomes extremely agitated and depressed anytime his plans fall through or somebody resists, or forgets, to do what he demands. Furthermore, Ego regularly attracts conflict and contradiction. S/he likes to control everybody and every situation and gets depressed often because controlling others and events are both difficult and unreasonable expectations. There are always arguments and clashes of Egos among individuals, leading to frustrating situations and the loss of a great deal of energy and productivity. Ego does not forgive and forget. He does not accept even an occasional submission, i.e., blaming himself instead of others. Every discussion, competition, battle, transaction, and simple matter that he is involved with has to end in a 'win' situation for him, but more importantly a loss for somebody else. When this is not the case, he gets anxious and depressed. In addition, since he is mainly preoccupied with 'winning and success' instead of 'learning and contribution,' he has a hard time exploring his self-actualization potentialities and needs. He may continue to win and feel successful, but also builds up a great deal of stress and anxiety, because he cannot internalize the meaning of a real achievement. He feels depressed and empty, in spite of all the symbols of winning and success surrounding him. His successes are not heartfelt and 'self' satisfying, because they are not selfless and authentic. S/he might hide or dismiss his/her inner conflicts and lack of deep satisfaction, but the depression of his/her psyche keeps building up. These are some of the major 'causes' of the self-induced depression for an Ego-driven personality.

The externally generated depression of Ego is similarly due to his expectations not being fulfilled and the clashes of his Ego with the demands, shortfalls, and Egos of other members of the society or organizations. He has a hard time having a simple conversation without the interference of Ego and an inevitable contradiction or clash.

Therefore, for Ego, the causes of both self-induced and externally induced depressions are also very much the same. They both result from expectations not met and competitions not won. His depression experiences are caused either when he is trying to exploit others and they resist (self-induced), or when others are imposing their own rules and expectations that do not appeal to him and thus become Ego-threatening (externally induced).

The 'feelings' of depression are severe and recur frequently due to the pressures on him/her to fulfil a wide range of his/her needs in peculiar ways through selfish schemes. Ego must make continuous efforts to push others for some (often unreasonable) goals, excel in everything, and win all the competitions, even when the rewards are not significant or the issues are not important. As these egotistical schemes and processes go on constantly, the rewards and disappointments are also recurring with a high frequency. The 'feelings' of fulfilment and depression are thus hitting him continuously based on the outcome of each experience. They are exhausting and depressing. It would be like a gambler becoming happy with every hand he wins and depressed with every hand he loses. At the end, the whole cycle of happiness-depression feelings becomes a nerve-racking loop and more of a stressful mechanism even when the cycle is at its height during a happiness experience. The psyche anticipates the depressions that may come tomorrow or the next second, and also remembers the depressions of yesterday(s).

The 'impact' of depression experiences and cycles on the person is obvious. The nervous breakdowns, neurosis, stress and heart attacks, which are sweeping us our feet in large numbers every day, are mostly the impacts of endless depression cycles and experiences caused by Ego. The 'effect' is also obvious. The amount of pressures we are putting on one another with our Egos continuously is simply killing our spirits, not to mention the stress and exhaustion they cause. In families, in work places, in our simplest transactions, and every time that we get into action or interact, our Egos interfere. What could we expect the 'effect' of a neurotic or overanxious person be on others, other than causing more damage to this vicious cycle of impacting self and affecting others adversely every day, to what disastrous end—only God may know.

The Depression of 'Self'

The self-induced depressions of Self are caused by his regrets about personal impurities that he is incapable of controlling while living in a chaotic environment. Self feels sad about the impurity of human nature, especially when friends and family members keep disappointing him more often than not. Self gets sad when he feels helpless in expressing himself and when his Model and Ego take charge temporarily, while Self feels obliged to keep them in check. We suffer, consciously or subconsciously, when Self, which is our conscience in this sense, fails to restrain Ego and Model. When our innocence is threatened, Self feels sad. When our potentialities are not effectively utilized, Self feels empty, unfulfilled and depressed. And when our spirituality needs are not satisfied, Self feels lonely, unprotected, helpless, and depressed.

The externally induced depressions come from the environments that Self is expected to adapt to. The realities of social living initially restrict the growth of Self. However, more importantly, these socioeconomic and political environments enforce the kind of value systems and conditions unacceptable to the integrity of Self. There is always a conflict between what these environments expect from a person and what his Self can submit to.

For both cases of self-induced and externally induced depressions, the 'causes' are merely the symptoms of social living that are mostly out of one's control. Yet, despite the limited power to induce change, Self has a much better capability to absorb the waves of depression without getting infected. While there are experiences of depression, the 'feelings' of depression are mild, infrequent, and manageable. This is because Self (that is perhaps partially aware due to a person's conscience) recognizes the 'causes' of depression as weaknesses of his personality (the Self in the process of development). Self realizes that these weaknesses are impossible to bypass and ignore completely due to the realities of social living. Self knows that these mild depressions are natural during the process of growth. During the transition from the *perceived* world to the *real* world—the process of cleansing our illusions—depressions are the results of our regrets for past mistakes and memories. We may never get the chance to become hundred percent purified as an absolute Self, which means some depressions always resurface due to our vulnerabilities and sense of human impurity. However, the intensity is low and Self is aware of its nature, cause, and healing effect. When Self knows the reasons of his depressions, he uses this information to heal itself rather than store it as a psychological hurt.

Therefore, for Self, even the impact of a depression experience is more of a learning and healing nature, rather than an obstacle for finding happiness experiences. We may say that the 'impacts' of a depression experience for Self are more positive than negative. In fact, these experiences may help the growth of Self, as they reinforce the process of self-control, creation, and meditation. During these periods, we learn a great deal about our true potentialities and creativity in line with our finer impressions of the universe, Nature, and our existence.

The 'effects' of depression experiences are at the very least neutral for a Self personality. Usually, a depression experience leads to a temporary withdrawal and meditation. During this period, Self does not deal with others and issues, but rather concentrates on the 'cause' and 'feeling' of the experience and tries to learn a lesson and build more stamina and creativity. Subsequent to a period of solitude, Self emerges with much more energy, compassion, and wisdom that can only have positive effects on others.

Depression experiences are too pervasive and powerful because they occur regularly to every aspect of personality separately or concurrently. We feel depressed too often because one or more of our personality aspects may be hurt at any time when its unique needs and urges are jeopardized. Depression experiences also have different implications for each of three aspects of personality in the long run. Model and Ego depressions have extreme repercussions on both the person himself and people around him. For Self, however, a depression cycle is mostly a learning and healing opportunity that keeps helping the person achieve his objective of Self-control faster.

One danger of depression lies in the fact that people do not understand its nature and source and thus have difficulty analysing it. Therefore, they simply suffer more and accept depression as a reality of living. A depression attack should in fact be viewed as a warning signal to pause and find its source realistically by relating it to a specific personality aspect and the underlying message coming from it. Understanding its source, internal or external, is important too.

The Happiness/Depression Cycles

The cycles of happiness and depression clash regularly and lead to additional personal frustration and stress. Even small events, e.g., someone's simple whining, spoils our mood and often even ends a happiness cycle prematurely. We feel these mood swings regularly and yet do not stop to grasp the important life lessons they offer. For one thing, we ignore the simple fact that controlling the sources of our ongoing, self-induced depressions is more important than looking for that elusive happiness. We forget that our own raw ambitions, obsessions, idiosyncrasies, phobia, and uptightness prevent us from feeling peace and happiness. We look for shallow pleasures to suffocate our depression instead of learning to understand the real source and message of any depression.

In Part III, we set out to explore the possibility of finding a meaningful and lasting formula of happiness. We are going to conclude here with the single note that, "Unless we build a 'self'-control mechanism to at least monitor our ongoing cycles of depression and assess their causes, the idea of finding happiness is obscure and unattainable." This is the bottom line, while a list of secondary points are offered on page 183-6.

The four elements of 'cause,' 'feeling,' 'impact,' and 'effect' of a happiness or depression experience determine its nature and longevity. Happiness experiences last when 'self' is dominant and we are free from our wicked thoughts and urges. Conversely, depression comes more often when we are serving the needs of Model and Ego.

Nonetheless, we face a major dilemma all our lives: On the one hand, we are limiting our chances for real happiness experiences by empowering Model and Ego beyond the minimum role they must play in a healthy lifestyle. We just do not see or care how they are keeping us from achieving happiness while we struggle with our greed-laden ambitions and fantasies. On the other hand, overcoming the urges of Model and Ego, especially in a crooked environment like ours, is surely not easy. We cannot grasp and revive the obscure, weakened Self quickly to fight off the wicked Ego and Model. We need self-awareness first and then patience, practice, evaluation, and growth. Only when we recognize Model and Ego as obstacles, we have a better chance of defeating them and revamping their roles in our lives and decisions.

Finding the ultimate happiness is an idealistic objective, anyway, and yet, we may get at least a glimpse of it if we can curb the incessant cycles of depression. This is a huge challenge, which makes ultimate happiness an extremely high expectation for common people who are driven mainly by their Models and Egos. We need an absolute 'self'-driven life and personality to escape the perils of the socioeconomic and political environments, and even so, it would be an impractical and imprudent practice. We cannot remain unaffected by the inefficiencies, ineffectiveness, corruptions, and abuses of socioeconomic systems and authorities that we elect to run our countries and communities. The entire democratic process is screwed up even in developed countries while the rich rules the means of controlling people's minds and votes. We have to get involved and we are eventually forced to play their games to defeat them when necessary. We cannot confront Model and Ego driven individuals merely by our Self. Our bureaucratic systems and organizations are also the exact replicas and representations of the 'model' and 'ego' personalities (the executives) that are running and controlling those organizations. We would be crushed quickly within the Ego-driven mechanisms and destroyed under the influence of Model oriented societies instantly. At best, we would be isolated and rejected. It is too late to be a Mahatma Gandhi or Nelsen Mandela.

Choosing and maintaining the right balance of personality aspects is a daunting personal issue and choice. We need to use enough Self to attain some level of happiness, and at the same time, we need some Model and Ego to help us survive in this chaotic social order. What is the right mix? How much should we be threatened and feel insecure by our basic survival needs, i.e., financial and economic pressures and organization demands, etc.? And how much happiness can we really bring to ourselves by leaning more toward our Self? These are major life decisions that we must make, particularly at the younger age, for building the foundation of our thoughts and life philosophy. We face these dilemmas throughout our lives, anyway. All along, we change our minds, preferences, and criteria regularly to adapt, and thus become more confused as we grow and learn about the meanings of survival and pleasure versus happiness.

The objective of happiness (peace of mind) is an integral part of our thoughts about life and living. Our discussions of happiness show how fragile the whole issue of life philosophy can be, considering the major contradiction between the path to happiness and the path of survival. It appears as if 'happiness' and the 'practicality of living' are opposing ideas that cannot be easily reconciled into a meaningful philosophy. Nonetheless, the possibility of happiness through 'self' exploration is a reality that we can depend on for developing the structure of our life philosophy.

We must stop doubting the fact that happiness is an intrinsic virtue of 'self' and that it is the only place we should look for happiness. We may then focus only on doubts and decisions about life practicalities, since they are stopping us from reaching a state of 'self'-hood and happiness. Within this framework, we can even entertain our deep belief (expectation) about deserving happiness as our legitimate right of being a *being*. Deserving happiness is perhaps a true claim if we can deal effectively with both our idiosyncrasies and the practicalities of living that create too many cycles of depression.

It is interesting to study our *mood* when we are neither happy nor depressed and thus appreciate its value for our welfare. What kind of a state is that? Contentment? A normal state? This study is beyond the scope of this book, although it seems that we live in that state more often than we are either happy or depressed. However, if somebody asks us how we feel at any moment, we suddenly lean toward a sense of satisfaction (happiness) or boredom (depression). This shows the deep state of our psyche regardless of our superficial feelings. Overall, maintaining a sense of contentment and mental stability over the long period would be blissful, but rather abnormal for human nature in general. Thus, as we move between happiness and depression moods rather frequently, we cause so much turmoil for our psyche. We overuse our nerves and drain our spirits. We cause our sufferings.

Depression and Suffering

We have the option of 'self'-therapy or seeking the assistance of experts to overcome the depression caused by our psychological defects, or Ego and Model. All we need is an initial awareness and honest assessment of our weaknesses, which cause our suffering. We can help ourselves if we really believe that some *adjustments* are necessary. However, most of the time, we really do not see our deficiencies or believe in our ability to overcome them.

Obviously, some sources of sufferings are more difficult to control. This usually happens when brain chemicals or external forces create or reinforce the sufferings. For example, financial burdens are always tangible and possibly due to no fault of our own. Even when caused by our defects such as laziness or extravagance, we still suffer, maybe even more, though at least we could try to do something about it. If we are reasonably aware, and make use, of our potentials to make a living, and do not waste our resources on unnecessary habits or ideas, then our financial hardship is probably not our fault. Or when we have difficulty with our relationships, it is often hard to adjust the situation. In most cases, it is also difficult to get out of them without causing a different kind of suffering for ourselves and others. Still, some alternatives may exist to alleviate the suffering. These kinds of unsolvable relationships can be worked out with some *adjustments* in our mentality and attitude when the situation itself cannot be rectified. Usually couples must find a more practical relationship model to help them interact more productively, even if it would have be a rather passive relationship.

We can choose a personal life path and develop a sensible mentality away from the influence of our lifelong biases and prejudices. A sound foundation of thoughts definitely shows us the need for passion and compassion, flexibility, stability, strengthening our beliefs, grasping 'self,' understanding the true means of happiness, and a life philosophy that inhibits sufferings. During this process, as our wisdom grows, we might gain some insights about life's mysteries, too, which would be only a sacred personal achievement, but never a definite and universal interpretation. Nobody can ever develop a satisfactory meaning for life.

Our sufferings, their causes, and our incessant search for a more peaceful means of living are merely the symptoms of our negligence to strive for self-awareness and the wisdom of a *'self'-control* life. Once we learn to live under the guidance of 'self,' according to the simple rules of the real world, we would not face as much suffering in our highly demanding societies. In the real world, beyond our demented illusions about life, our wisdom would be sufficient to void the sources, and avoid the thoughts, of suffering. We would be able to anticipate the situations, thoughts, and feelings of suffering. We may even be able to turn them around to our advantage in the form of passion and compassion, which are usually the main keys for discovering a few basic things about the big mysteries of life.

We can readily grasp and relate to the common sources of sufferings. However, some deep causes of sufferings are due to the deprivation of our inner needs, including spirituality. This happens when we neglect to place sufficient emphasis on significant matters of life and to relinquish the majority of nonsensical desires, ambitions, plans, thoughts, actions, and decisions that we have been emphasizing on uselessly.

Our psyches are burdened by various sources of suffering from early on in our lives when we grow within, and adopt, many crooked social values. For example, a child may show great frustration and suffering when one of his grades is not high enough or if he is not getting enough attention at school from his classmates and teachers. His conventional thinking (and sense of competition) makes him feel inadequate when he feels unappreciated or when he gets any grade lower than 'A,' because he has established it as a criterion for self-worth. These kinds of experiences feel like major failure or rejection and valid excuses for suffering. Only through some kind of mental rewiring and creativity, he can unlearn the condition of giving the matter of competition such significance. He needs a better criterion for success in order to avoid unnecessary sufferings all his life. Instead, we all absorb and apply these crude criteria for the rest of our lives so naively.

A fundamental cause of suffering is loneliness. The impression of loneliness hurts many people all by itself, even if they are only slightly ignored or when they are alone just a few hours. They are simply not prepared to bear even temporary loneliness, or even the impression of it. Obviously, many options exist nowadays for groups or individuals to work together to alleviate their sufferings due to loneliness. However, learning about the positive side of loneliness can reduce our fears of it, too, at least partially. During our no-thought experiences, we learn how moments of solitude (loneliness) could be relaxing and peaceful. Naturally, loneliness on a long-term basis is more complex than occasional ones. However, we can create some no-thought experiences to inhibit loneliness sufferings, learn some self-reliance, and perhaps induce higher consciousness and exceptionally divine feelings.

Drawing upon the sacred energy and passion that a no-thought state or loneliness creates, we can satisfy our deeper needs, which automatically generate tranquility and freedom. In those moments and conditions, we can create beautiful things and thoughts that override the feelings of loneliness many folds. The only problem is that our fears and conventional view of loneliness do not allow us to test and appreciate the advantages of solitude. We have become so desperately attached to things and other people, and, as a result, developed this tremendous paranoia and phobia about loneliness. Yet, in the real world, in fact, we are alone and stay lonely, even if we have a house full of friends and family. This does not mean that socializing is unimportant, but rather to recognize the merits of solitude early on in our lives. A more important point here is that the fear of loneliness can be cured only by discovering the joy of many life experiences that erupt only from loneliness and are extremely beautiful and full of passion.

Sufferings due to boredom relates to the lack of self-fulfilment. It reflects our negligence to find our niche and developing it. We all have some hidden potentials that press us subconsciously to emerge. They demand our attention or else we feel unfulfilled and empty. Exploring and nurturing our potentialities is difficult. However, once developed, they provide a chance for both 'self'-actualization and personal growth, which are the best antidote for sufferings too. These adventures are merely for internal gratification with no other ulterior motives. These experiences fill our lives with joy and creative energy, which would subdue our stress and banal sufferings due to boredom.

If our suffering relates to greed and jealousy, then it should be obvious how we can get rid of it. Why do we continue to look for more of the same things, which we cannot consume in our lifetime anyway, is difficult to grasp. How much wealth and power is enough? We can only ask our Ego! This only shows the absence of a reliable foundation of thoughts to guide our lives.

CHAPTER THIRTEEN
The Philosophy of Happiness

Now we know some truths about the mystery of happiness. We know that the four elements of happiness must be potent in a continuous cycle of personal experiences that satisfy our Self rather than feed our Ego and Model. Now, our attempts to find happiness through wealth and power may appear not too potent for Self-realization, after all. Therefore, now, we must reassess our customary views of happiness and establish a more sensible mentality and lifestyle.

We have always imagined that by solving the mysteries of life and love, the secret of happiness unfolds readily. However, our struggles to find the meaning of life for reaching at least some inner peace have led to no tangible results. Our craving to conquer love for a lasting happiness in the arms of a companion has also brought us only more disappointments. Now, we know that life has no particular meaning or purpose and love is an extremely tenuous experience that can never satisfy Self or feed the four basic elements of happiness. Now, we know that we may find happiness within ourselves mostly in the form of contentment and wisdom. Now, we know that 'positive thinking' per se or 'living in the now' casually cannot lead to happiness. We know, now, that we need a proactive mind, a personal life philosophy, and a simple lifestyle to master the mystery of happiness.

Along with this general formula for exploring happiness, we need a thought process and approach to support our efforts. As noted in Chapter One, our thoughts are often about happiness: What is it, and how we should go about finding it? On the one hand, only self-awareness and purposeful thoughts enrich our lives and lead us to find happiness according to a personal life philosophy. On the other hand, these philosophical thoughts can cause disappointment and stress when solutions are rare, while life's reality also keeps getting harsher, against our divine desires.

Unfortunately, a large amount of our thoughts (both fundamental and trivial) causes stress and depletes our energy and spirits. All along, we spend most of our waking hours wondering about our needs, sufferings, and remedies, either consciously or subconsciously. We seek all kinds of pleasures in hopes of feeling happy or eluding reality to at least subdue our sufferings. Eventually, mental pressures get overwhelming, as we do not know how to go about controlling the contents of our thoughts. Especially when our thoughts are not pleasant, motivating, or purposeful, they only hamper our ability to assess our decisions and actions sensibly. They only cause more doubts about the meaning of our actions and the purpose of living altogether. In all, our struggles to find happiness often lead to more distress, depression, and desperation due to our debilitating mentality and thoughts. However, now we at least have a general idea about the approach and requirements of finding happiness, if we can first find the courage and stamina that this adventure requires.

We may alleviate the repercussion of futile thoughts in two ways: First, we could build a general life philosophy to direct and harmonize the contents of our trivial thoughts, and to manage the level of activities that induce such confusing thoughts. Second, we could attempt routinely to give ourselves a break from thinking and allow our minds to only feel things, or, on some occasions stop thinking and feeling altogether—like the time we get into a deep meditation.

For creating a 'no-thought state,' we must learn to relieve our minds from trivial thoughts, which usually revolve around our needs, plans, and stress. In a no-thought state, we find peace and freedom, which is the same goal we have for building our life philosophy with a diligent (active) mind. Therefore, the question is how often we should force our minds to relax partially or totally, if we can control it, instead of thinking proactively and deeply for building or monitoring our life philosophy.

On the one hand, we expect our minds to be always sharp and alert for defending ourselves, and to be in constant control of our actions and decisions. We also need a sharp mind as part of our ongoing self-awareness exercises and for keeping life trivialities out of our minds. On the other hand, too much thinking and planning is driving most of us to the verge of insanity in an environment that hardly anything makes sense anymore. Thus, it becomes essential to find the right timing and ways for subduing our thoughts and quieting our mind as often and prudently as we can. Forcing a right balance between the above two approaches (i.e., keeping our mind in full alert versus total quiet) provides the best results, of course.

This paradoxical situation manifests as another integral characteristics of living, in line with our irreconcilable doubts, dilemmas, and inner conflicts. It presents another mystery of life. The foundation of our thoughts is formed around similar dichotomies, such as destiny versus planning, doubts versus decisions, facts versus myths, perceived versus real world, challenges versus suffering, life versus death, 'self'-control versus practical personality, independence versus dependence, socializing versus solitude, etc. Nevertheless, we must somehow learn to use the right meaning, mix, and balance for each of these dichotomies. Subsequently, we must find a philosophical framework to reconcile all of them collectively when necessary, too. This total paradox seems to be the underlying property of life and thus the foundation of our thoughts as we navigate in the ocean of uncertainties forever. Reaching that collective balance in our lives unravels the mysteries of life and happiness.

At the same time, we may think of our foundation of thoughts as an intelligent engine with many complementary and refined (but also clashing) parts that should work together for the ultimate objective of running a volatile machine called human. Making an efficient engine for running an instable machine is not easy but necessary. Obviously, when the engine is not balanced and strong, it would not provide adequate efficiency and output. Some parts may not function well from time to time, like when we have our doubts or face sudden dilemmas. Yet, we have the responsibility of identifying the problem and repairing the part, so the engine can return to full efficiency. The engine requires regular checkups and tune-ups, like the times we need to stop our thought processes and quiet our minds. The engine might boil sometimes like the times when anger and Ego dominate us. In those moments, we should just slow down and stop for a while to let the engine cool down.

The foundation of our thoughts will serve as an engine in pursuit of special objectives and decisions of life. These fundamental thoughts, in conjunction with our real life experiences, make up our 'primary wisdom,' which includes our outlook on life, personality, and the means and methods of handling life matters, including our major life decisions and actions. An efficient and sophisticated engine is needed to drive our decisions and actions in the journey of life. We need a solid engine to withstand life turbulences and get us to our destiny as smoothly and safely as we deserve. We do not want any major regrets or breakdowns because of our naive mishandling of the engine.

This is how we envision the operation of our thoughts. Yet, this is only one function of our thoughts. The foundation of our thoughts is much more complex and we cannot consider it solely an engine to run our decisions and actions for reaching some level of happiness. Beyond its application to our worldly affairs, the foundation of our thoughts should also help us find a true vision of life and our spiritual link to the universe. We have realized that our thoughts help us with life, but more importantly, it should transcend us beyond all the worldly decisions and actions. It should help us understand, believe in, and find a path of wisdom deserving the dignity of human beings in the form we have evolved. We may find tranquility now that happiness is impossible to sustain. We may even reach a higher morality considering our intelligence and the long history of 'thinking humans' looking for salvation. We need a strong foundation of thoughts to help us transcend to other domains and territories not sketched on the one-dimensional maps of the perceived world. These discoveries are the most important functions for our thoughts, but unfortunately, we have so far failed to use them for mitigating human suffering as a whole.

Managing Our Thoughts

Most of our thoughts are mechanical, mundane, erratic, daydreaming, and often stressful. They are caused by hallucinations, paranoia, misperceptions, and personal idiosyncrasies in general. However, we also strive intuitively to manage our thoughts in order to be effective, happy, objective, and avoid the stress of needless musing. We would like to manage our thoughts for three purposes:
1. To better understand and support our inner needs, life decisions, and actions.
2. To develop and maintain a personal life philosophy and find a path of wisdom to reach contentment and peace of mind.
3. To stop our thoughts and give our minds a chance to rest, and our souls an opportunity to relax and heal.

Managing our thoughts implies our ability to manoeuvre effectively within the above three states regularly in order to minimize our preoccupation with all those mundane, liquid thoughts (the 80-90 percent portion). Our success depends on our character and background, but also personal efforts to control our thoughts at least thirty percent of the time. Even this minimal awareness of our thoughts is helpful for maintaining a healthier lifestyle. We spend a reasonable amount of time on decisions and actions related to our normal daily activities (purpose number 1 above). But aside from that, we merely waste our lives on soft thoughts like daydreaming, reminiscing our past experiences, and struggling with our paranoia and other psychological defects, including jealousy, spite, and competition.

With these types of raw and liquid thoughts, we develop more unmanaged expectations and unauthentic needs, which lead to further psychological deprivations and defects. We suffer unnecessarily and worry uselessly. Sometimes, we even create disruptive thoughts with no foundation or relation to our physical or psychological needs, but rather driven by our anger, spite, paranoia, or desire for vengeance. These futile thoughts directly inflict us with pain and confusion and sabotage our nervous system that explodes eventually. So, most of us need a plan (consciousness) to re-distribute our thinking habits and energy to minimize the soft thoughts and instead cover the purposes 2 and 3 noted above in a more balanced and routine manner.

Managing our thoughts means controlling the types of ideas that we allow into our heads. We restrict troubling thoughts that have little or no consequence in the end. We rely on our primary wisdom to set our life priorities and make our major life decisions effectively away from personal whims and the pressures imposed on us in complex socioeconomic environments. The time we spend on enhancing the foundation of our thoughts through meditation and reading is never too much. Studying the ideas and prophecies of thinkers and philosophers enforces and supports personal thoughts and individual creativity.

Finally, we must learn how to meditate and create the moments of no-thought, and how much. A no-thought state also occurs by consciously freeing our minds from musing. We could instead amuse ourselves with life experiences (hobbies) that do not require serious decisions and thinking, but provide only feelings of joy, discovery, and satisfaction.

The Formula of Happiness

The discussions in Part III show why prescribing a particular 'formula of happiness' would always remain a tentative attempt at best. It is difficult to establish a standard or criterion for real happiness due to many factors. For one thing, individuals' perceptions and unique mix of personality aspects (i.e., Model, Ego, Self) make their expectations and approaches in life different. Accordingly, their definitions of happiness vary based on their needs and deprivations. Moreover, happiness experiences are unique in intensity and length, too. These obstacles and many other factors make the practicality of finding and applying a fixed 'formula of happiness' questionable. Yet, we all hope to unravel this mystery, too, along with many other life puzzles.

Ultimately, happiness is an abstract perception that eludes a comprehensive definition. The best definition that we can invent for common purpose is that 'happiness' is the outcome of profound experiences that impact a person's soul deeply, improve his outlook on life, which then affect others positively too.

Nonetheless, the following general guidelines can be derived from the discussions in the last two chapters regarding the characteristics of happiness:

1. Happiness is not a phenomenon out there that can be defined and accessed independent from the personality of the person experiencing it. An individual cannot pursue a path of happiness outside himself and without making substantial changes to his/her own personality and outlook on life.
2. Contrary to common perception, we do not deserve happiness as long as we expect to find it within our pervasive, crooked lifestyles and shallow mentality.
3. Pleasures can at best replicate only a short sense of happiness. They do not cause happiness or eradicate depression.
4. Happiness is an intrinsic property of 'self.' Thus, it can be automatically generated from within us, without too much effort. All we need is a simple knowledge of how the prin-

ciples of happiness work within 'self,' and how they can be nurtured in our minds. The first principle, of course, is to minimize the roles of Model and Ego in our lives. The challenge is to believe in, and activate, as much of the 'self' aspect of our personality as we are capable of accessing and using. We must monitor our actions, reactions, communications, and encounters to gauge the influence of Model, Ego, and Self, as well as the motivations behind them. Ultimately, we must learn to become a better human being.

5. We should view happiness as a flower blossoming from the plant of personality. The same way a plant must be observed and fed with nutrients to support its flowering properties, a person's personality aspects must be constantly monitored and balanced to enhance one's capacity for happiness. A mature personality has the properties of a year-round flowering plant, where everlasting happiness manifests as an intrinsic property of one's unique personality. Thus, happiness is automatic when the personality is well groomed. Yet, explaining any happiness experience is like describing the beauty of a particular flower that has its own unique properties and fragrance.

6. Happiness requires high self-awareness. Not only the prevalence of 'self' is required for cultivating the plant of happiness, but also special attention to the properties of the flower itself is necessary. We should train ourselves to be aware of the happiness of our 'self,' the same way we look at the flowers of a particular plant consciously and enjoy it. If flowers are not healthy and strong, we assess the situation and adjust the watering, fertilizing, or change the environment (the soil) of the plant. In the same manner, the happiness of 'self' has to be monitored and personality adjustment be made to correct any signs of lethargy in the intensity of 'self' driven happiness. The awareness of 'self' is discussed briefly in this book. It simply means remembering 'who we are,' 'what the purpose of our living is,' and the

whole vulnerability of our lives leading to the inevitable death. Being conscious of our physical health as well as our psychological growth are other means of 'self'-awareness. We also need to have 'self'-control over our physical and psychological needs (i.e., social and inner temptations) to avoid mental deprivation or stagnation.

7. A real happiness experience has four elements (characteristics). It has a legitimate and worthwhile 'cause,' it generates authentic 'feelings' of inner joy and completeness, it 'impacts' the person in a meaningful and deep way, and as a result, the person can 'affect' other individuals, events, and things in a positive way as well. For lasting happiness, we should pursue mostly those experiences that can entail all these four elements fully. Accordingly, the cycles of happiness should be continuous and deep.

8. Happiness cannot rely on external sources and whims. The events and experiences causing happiness are only important to the extent they can create the four elements of happiness regularly. Therefore, small experiences that can be attained quite readily are potentially more powerful in steering and generating happiness experiences. For example, the joy of gardening is something that, once appreciated, can become a major source of real happiness and 'self' growth. When we explore the details of a good piece of music, especially classical music for those who like it, we discover simple and small notes and creations every time we listen to it. For music and art, even though somebody else has done the creation aspect of it, we still appreciate and associate with the genius that has gone into it and enjoy it with high intensity. We can repeat the experience of listening to the music or viewing the arts that reinforce the cycles of happiness experiences in our lives. We can make a habit of producing those simple experiences that keep the cycles of happiness running perpetually and smoothly. When it comes to our own creations, the intensity of happiness caused by these

achievements and self-actualizing experiences is ten folds higher. It makes great sense to score individual achievements, i.e., arts, inventions, and other ventures that enrich our lives and propagate the intensity of our happiness experiences by affecting other humans too.

9. Happiness runs parallel with the level of personal potentialities realized. Following our dreams, when they are supported by our realistic recognition of our potentialities and abilities, has a good chance of leading to happiness experiences. Conversely, following some erratic dreams, solely based on false pretences, hope, positive thinking, or according to our deceptive perceptions of our potentialities, would most likely lead to stagnation and depression experiences.

10. Happiness experiences are much more frequent and rewarding once we choose and follow a path of wisdom with a fixed life philosophy. Abolishing the sources of our gullibility, e.g., our blind submission to religions, positive thinking gimmicks, or baseless spirituality regiments, is the first step toward wisdom and happiness. In our search, we learn about the other dimensions of our 'self,' including our spirituality urge. Accordingly, we not only learn about our ignored potentialities, but also access inner energies that would free us from the limitations of a mere physical existence.

11. Happiness cycles are less frequently interrupted when we learn to recognize and avoid the traps of depression cycles. When 'self' induces depression, e.g., our sadness about human impurity, the experience should be used for learning, healing, compassion, and creating.

12. Happiness cycles are intensified when we learn to pause and ponder our rational doubts about objects, people, and events. Through this awareness process, we develop a personal life philosophy to deal with reality, make the right life decisions, and fulfil our responsibilities effectively.

CHAPTER FOURTEEN
Forward Thinking Philosophy

We need a sound and practical personal life philosophy to direct our efforts for self-awareness and finding at least contentment, and maybe even happiness. Yet, we must first adopt a general life philosophical platform, such as 'forward thinking,' which appeals to this author.

Forward thinking is a philosophical notion to set our life priorities and outlook according to the three fundamental questions everybody faces in the three life phases. The idea is to view life's essentialities based on our future wisdom after years of living and experiencing all aspects of life. Logically, the information content and value of our experiences are cumulative and thus our wisdom increases with age. Especially, our mentality, priorities, and outlook on life improve. (This is a plausible assumption for most people, as long as one's mental health is intact and before aging ruins a person's sense of judgment and reasoning.) Overall, we may assume that our wisdom in the third phase of life is more valuable and reliable than the one we have in the earlier phases. Yet, we believe to be the smartest person in the world during adolescence. We are usually most arrogant and stubborn about our viewpoints when we are least experienced, most impatient, too passionate, and quite vulnerable. In a way, we can say that almost all our helplessness and sufferings in life are the price we end up paying for our stubbornness and naivety during the earlier phases of our lives, especially the first one.

The wisdom and insight at each phase of life depends on person's intelligence and thought processes. Yet, by the third phase of our lives, we have faced almost all the doubts and decisions of life, made many mistakes and adjustments to our thoughts and attitudes, experienced the pleasures of life, and perhaps learned something about our spirituality and actualization needs. We are more realistic about our dreams and have leaned more toward our Self, since Ego and Model cannot serve us as much as before. We finally realize the value of Self for bringing us peace and tranquility. We grow deeper insight about life's essentialities and meaning. We learn to come to terms with ourselves and reach for our souls instead of pursuing many superficial goals. Unless our life outlook and values are too negative and dark due to severe life hardships and failures, a normal person learns objectivity and gains wisdom as s/he ages.

Our intention for forward thinking is to listen to the depth of the messages that people in their third phase of life convey about life by thinking or asking the question of, 'What was it all about?' There is no specific advice in this phrase, but only a fundamental and philosophical expression about life in line with a better understanding of our social values' vanity. All we need is attention and basic trust in the messages that come from the simple phrase, 'What was it all about?' However, if it is the wisdom in the third phase of life that we want to 'forward-think,' we must also adjust our misperception of old people and their wisdom. We must actually gain the capacity to imagine ourselves as an old person very soon and asking the same question.

As a young person, however, we dissociate ourselves from older people and their values. We cannot even grasp the concept of getting old and fragile ourselves consciously. Ironically, even people in their middle or old ages put a distance between elderly and themselves, desperately hoping to come across young and alert. Youths are too proud of their fresh and youthful values and outlook on life to even listen to any elderly wisdom. Our subconscious fear of death also makes us feel anxious around older people. All that traditional respect for the wisdom of the elderly has been eradicated in the new eras due to the fast rise of arrogance and superficiality. Obviously, some of the general perceptions about the values and viewpoints of older people is valid, since with old age come senility, depression, and health issues. Often, these factors make an older person's judgments less trustworthy and more depressing than usual. However, while they still have their senses intact, old people's question of, 'What was it all about?' is a reliable conclusion about the frailty and shallowness of life. Unfortunately, most people, especially elderly, cannot articulate their feelings and wisdom. However, they are all thinking the points noted in this chapter, at least subconsciously. We can see it in their faces anyway.

The three philosophical questions listed on page 65 have passed the test of history and would remain valid forever, because the overall human nature would not change anyway. We like to make life miserable for one another and we are not made to get along for a long time. Therefore, hardships, exploitations, and agonies of life would continue forever and the three fundamental questions in the three phases of life would stay intact. We can be certain that these three questions become even more pertinent in the future while societies continue to deteriorate so fast. We could verify the validity of these questions in any era by talking to people in different phases of their lives and capable of speaking intelligently and honestly. We can expect the same outcome even though we might believe that time has changed, we are more modern, and we are wiser.

Of course, nobody should rely on the wisdom of one person or group for building his/her life philosophy, anyway. While a specific individual's wisdom is valuable if we trust his/her faculty, our interest is mainly in uniform messages of a large group of thoughtful people in the third phase of their lives who have proven their high intelligence and impartiality, perhaps as scholars and philosophers. Meanwhile, we can also check with normal people in the latter phases of their lives and see how prevalent the main life messages are among the public at all levels of intelligence and lifestyles.

Forward thinking is mainly a hypothetical thought at this point. Maybe someday—in the 50th century perhaps—humans develop some magical techniques to foretell their future thoughts and states of mind. However, for now, we may use this hypothetical idea only to enhance our awareness, and to inject some doubts in our minds about the essentialities of life as we see them nowadays in our *presumably modern* cultures. We cannot realistically expect youth to think like their parents, let alone their grandparents, or really feel and understand the wisdom that comes only from actual experiences. All we can do, as intended here too, is to open their thought horizons to give a benefit of a doubt to the collective wisdom of people who all ask the same question, 'What was it all about?'

When we are young in the first phase of our lives, we are full of ambitions, plans, and need for pleasures. This is a natural attitude and expectation to the extent it corresponds with our instincts and basic needs. Beyond this primary intuition, our attitudes and thoughts reflect the conditioning norms, materialistic standards, and pleasure-seeking priorities of the modern society that we learn to imitate. We have turned into robots who follow the crowd and social trends with very little 'self'-control on the process and direction of our lives, although we strongly believe that we are independent and in charge. In this phase of life, as a young person, we are both naive and proud. We want to try our own ways and values, but at the same time, deep down in our unconscious, we feel committed to follow some standard life plans. We usually allow these standards and plans direct the path of our lives. We have some ideas about independence and breaking away, but at the same time, the criteria of success and the fake essentialities of life keep us trapped within a preset structure of life. They are the same values that all generations seem to adopt at each phase of life—the kind of mentality that keeps them totally dependent on their superficial habits and pretentious people around them—except that shallowness is increasing fast with every generation. In the first life phase, we are optimistic about future, sometimes even despite our cynicism about life. We think that we are smart and capable of making things happen for us, money, love, and fame, and everything else that we accept and admire as the criteria of success.

The main characteristic of this phase is the attitude of forward looking (not 'forward thinking') and wondering *what our lives would be like.* The essentialities of life are set with the same criteria that we have used to delineate the formula of success. In fact, in our minds, success and happiness are synonymous. Most likely, we do not even dwell on happiness and the factors leading to it, because we imagine that success brings happiness automatically—a major assumption that proves to be wrong in the second and third phases of our lives. Meanwhile, we fill our lives with short-term pleasures just to keep ourselves amused, and because everybody else is doing the same stuff. The path of life in the eyes of youth is quite clear. It consists of having more pleasures (for replicating happiness) while striving for, and looking forward to, more future success.

Our cultures define 'success' only in terms of materialistic criteria. Our immediate perception of the word 'success' is money, luxuries, power, fame, sexuality, and extravagance. What we do to get to this point does not matter, and what we feel even when we are there still does not matter. All we are used to perceive and measure is one's level of wealth and fame as valid ends all by themselves. Automatically, we associate these symbols of success directly to an absolute definition of success and conclude quickly about a person's degree of success and happiness. In fact, we have become so naive and conditioned that when we are told that an individual is not happy despite his wealth and fame, we get extremely surprised.

Strangely enough, we reject the idea that a person is actually not successful because he is not happy (despite his money and power). That is, we assume readily that if somebody is successful, according to our cultural standards, he should be happy, but not the opposite (as noted in the previous sentence). Naively, we insist that this person is really successful, but unable to appreciate it or be happy. Facing such a perceptually untenable and paradoxical situation, we then struggle to change our position and assume that happiness is something that we can buy with our success, rather than being an inherent state of satisfaction erupting from 'real' success. We try idiotically to redefine the relationship between success and happiness. So, even in our minds and perceptions, we are inconsistent in relating happiness and success. Although 'success' and 'happiness' are synonym in our common perceptions, we readily refute their relationship when someone's happiness does not materialize despite his success. Therefore, the only justification we offer to reconcile this inconsistency is that he does not know how to buy happiness with his success.

Success, as defined and recognized through various social symbols, and in the way we have imposed it upon ourselves in our cultures, is in fact more synonymous with suffering than happiness. We suffer a lot emotionally and physically by working so many hours and worrying about our profits and competitions, and at the end, all we can show for it is stress, loneliness, and defeated Egos. Even when we achieve our objectives of winning the competitions and making our wealth at any cost, we find our success to be at best only a business target; once we reach that target we have to shoot for a higher one. In the midst of all these struggles for success (higher targets), we become increasingly ignorant about the real meanings and sources of happiness, while hypnotically believe that we are happy or it would happen soon.

In all, we have spread a major misperception in our culture about success. Accordingly, we have conditioned ourselves, particularly in the earlier phases of our lives, to follow bizarre objectives and lifestyles for becoming successful and happy. Forward thinking is for reassessing these old habits and crooked social values regarding success and happiness. We should adjust our thoughts on this important issue.

Three important points must be clarified here:
1. Throughout the three phases of life, we all seek various forms of pleasure to mitigate our sufferings temporarily. This may even turn into an addiction if we believe that worrying, planning, or thinking about life is not a worthwhile strategy. We strive to 'live in the now' as much as possible. Building this type of easygoing mentality and a sense of irresponsibility is not the intention of 'forward thinking' philosophy.
2. Although 'Forward Thinking' messages discussed in this chapter might initially sound negative and depressing, their ultimate intention is to increase our chance for happiness (or at least contentment) by seeing life in a more realistic perspective. This important point is further explained below.
3. A young person who feels the futility of life must realize that s/he is in a special state of mind that could happen to anybody at any age or phase of life. These feelings are unrelated (or sometimes only auxiliary) to the main theme of 'forward thinking' and philosophical thoughts that majority of us hold in each phase of life. The point is that our outlook on life, e.g., its futility in the context of present socioeconomic systems, must be based on philosophical thoughts and wisdom, and not out of laziness, habit, or even intense suffering.

Phase Three Reference

The ultimate question of 'What was this life all about?' strikes us severely in the third phase of our lives. Thus, the idea behind the simple philosophy of 'forward thinking' is to familiarize ourselves with this inevitable late discovery at the beginning of our lives. Then we may consider adjusting our mentality and plans according to this cruel reality. There are many profound messages in this ultimate question, such as:

- We would all face and sense the question of, 'What was it all about?' when we reach the third phase of our lives.
- We would feel disappointment, and doubt our wisdom all along, throughout previous stages of our lives, regarding our futile worries and struggles for success.
- Life is indeed too short, even shorter than what we keep hearing and imagining.
- Our criteria of success and its outcome do not prove useful and meaningful, but rather quite irrelevant for reaching even a relative sense of happiness.
- The outcome of our plans often turns out differently.
- Our judgments about life and people change.
- We sense the absurdity of positive thinking.
- We realize our naïveté to trust certain values, thoughts, and criteria of success and happiness.
- We feel major regrets, helplessness, and sadness for the loss of an otherwise beautiful life.
- We feel the ultimate below—that there is no hope of escape from our present trap or much left to do.
- We finally accept that we are alone in this life regardless of all the friends and family surrounding us.
- We throw in the towel and accept our eventual resignation, defeat, and desperation.

Obviously, these messages are in fact too harsh to adopt as a reality of life, especially for young people who are just blooming with all kinds of optimism and enthusiasm. How can we tell them about the sad reality that would prove to be the *truth*, but sounds too depressing and negative? And even if we tried, how can we expect them to understand the depth of the messages wholeheartedly without giving up on life? The intention of the messages is most likely not even clear to us. It is easy to misinterpret these messages and believe that they are intended to portray the futility of life and our struggles to succeed. However, this is not the intention.

The real purpose of exposing ourselves to these messages is only to raise our awareness. In fact, the purpose is to see the futility of wasting our lives on those petty things and plans that we have learned to consider essential for success. The ultimate purpose is to obtain the highest level of satisfaction from life, find the real means of achieving happiness, and see the beauty of the real world. The interpretation of the messages must be based on an initial understanding of the purpose of 'forward thinking.' The main idea is to prepare ourselves for the inevitable shocks in life and thus sail through this journey as smoothly as possible with minimum scars, regrets, and expectations. Furthermore, the idea is not to encourage 'living in the now' more actively. On the contrary, a main objective of forward thinking is to plan our lives diligently by identifying and monitoring life's essentialities every single day.

The messages must motivate us to adjust our thoughts, attitudes, and actions to abandon the phony values and hollow lifestyles in the perceived world. Initially, the messages may appear counterproductive for setting the right values for our life challenges and struggles. They may create even greater doubts about the purpose of living and keeping ourselves amused with work, all kinds of pleasures, etc. We would probably get confused when no substantive joys and goals seem to come from following the forward thinking messages. What should our new values be if we now must consider social norms and values unimportant or at least questionable? These are legitimate concerns. However, we can overcome these hurdles if we contemplate the forward thinking messages along with the fundamental notions within the foundation of our thoughts, our philosophy, and primary wisdom. With the help of our foundation of thoughts, we replace any old and unessential value with more meaningful convictions and experiences. The process of adjusting our thoughts, attitudes, and actions is for the sake of a smooth transition from the old way of living and acting to the new ones. How we can make youth interested in this type of mentality—to abandon at least the excessive aspects of their pleasure-seeking desires—is an extremely tough job, though, if possible at all! The idea is not to abandon our social values and ways completely, but only adjust them for a more meaningful path of life.

Many other aspects of the 'forward thinking' can also be studied. For example, the messages of forward thinking reflect that all of our struggles and efforts to boost our Ego would prove futile and funny. At the end, our fat Ego would burst and we would see the emptiness of it all, not to mention our sense of stupidity. Therefore, once we adjust our attitudes, we learn to remain indifferent to suggestions or offences that our Ego usually would not tolerate, like somebody telling us that we are 'wrong' about something. Under normal condition, we spend a lot of energy and time to fight back and prove that we are not 'wrong.' We learn that, in the final analysis, from the viewpoint of forward thinking, it does not really matter whether somebody thinks we are right or wrong as long as we maintain an objective view of our thoughts and deeds. Only our objectivity and integrity matter in life, not other people's opinions. Our only goal is to find the means of staying objective, which is mainly useful for keeping our sanity and peace of mind.

With forward thinking, we would find it much easier to curb our fears and insecurities about the love we do not receive, the jobs we cannot find or promotions we do not get, the wealth we have not accumulated, etc. We can better control our anger about losing our spouse who proves to be extremely insensitive and ignorant, and when we realize how s/he disregards or misunderstands our love, etc. We can witness and withstand our kids' wickedness, cruelty, and apathy. We can see that our shallow senses of success, even when achieved, do not give us mental satisfaction and true happiness, i.e., peace of mind. We realize that not only those accomplishments are not the essentialities of life to be overly concerned about or lose our energies on, but also we realize how such alleged essentialities only heighten our fears and entrapments. Instead, we seek our sensible beliefs and real essentialities of life by setting better priorities and building our foundation of thoughts.

Phase Two Reference

The question, 'What is this (life about)?', which hits us in the second phase of life, also provides some great messages. The question implies that we are right in the middle of a mess and feel trapped. However, in this phase of life we are still hopeful and believe to be clever enough to escape the traps. We still believe there are ways to get out of this situation and things would eventually start to make sense. We think we might have done something wrong that could be corrected, e.g., by getting a divorce and finding a new spouse. We are still assuming that the same criteria and foundation of thoughts that we have followed so far are good enough to rescue us from our present entrapments. We still think of success and happiness in the same way and according to the same criteria. The question of, 'What is this?' contains the following messages:

- We are facing a major flaw in our plans and perceptions of life, as we had envisioned and eagerly adopted in the first phase of our lives.
- We are truly surprised to face such harsh outcomes at the prime of our lives.
- We feel the mess we are in and our entrapments in a serious way.
- We become anxious and frustrated, and do not understand why our plans, logic, and common sense do not work.
- We doubt the validity of our criteria of success, and thus the presumed automatic happiness.
- We notice the social chaos and people's hypocrisy more clearly and feel sad about the whole situation.

- We are still confused about the meaning of our experiences and remain doubtful regarding the real sources of our problems. Yet, we do not seem to have any other options open to us. So, we feel obliged to follow the same path and values to rectify the issues.
- At the same time, we blame our past mistakes and wonder whether we could find a way to correct them.
- We also blame others and bad luck for our failures, but we sometimes feel our naivety and dip into self-pity.
- We question our lifestyles with deeper doubts about the meaning and purpose of everything happening around us.
- The lingering sense of questioning things and reflecting—'What is this'—keeps intensifying. We do not know who to trust and where to turn for guidance.
- While we look for alternatives to get out of this mess, we seem helpless, as our dilemmas feel quite serious and overwhelming.
- We have all kinds of doubts about our future and our options, while none of those options seems viable. Still we force ourselves to push forward and we hope for a more manageable future. (It is only in the third phase of our lives that we lose our doubts and hopes, and finally believe in the frailty and shallowness of our dreams altogether.)
- We face the biggest doubt of our lives and keep asking ourselves: 'Is this what life supposed to be?'
- Yet, we still try to remain somewhat optimistic and keep looking for a solution despite our cynicism about the bizarre manifestation of life.
- We just get deeper in the same old habits, e.g., working harder and seeking more pleasures, for dealing with the tough dilemmas erupting in this life phase.

The question, 'What is this?', in the phase two of life shows that a big part of the optimism and enthusiasm of phase one diminishes and a sense of reality kicks in. We face the walls of resistance, disappointments, and discouragements. Definitely, some beautiful experiences of life keep us going. Some moments and experiences of happiness and pleasures partly make up for our depressions, delusions, and confusions. However, we realize on a grand scale how those perceptions of happy life and success have been a deceiving mirage. They only look promising and satisfying from a distance when we are in Phase One, but are empty and elusive when we actually reach them and touch them in Phase Two. They are boring at best.

The main, shocking finding in Phase Two is about our view of success and happiness. We realize that we have no realistic set of criteria outside the conditioning and restricted social norms. We realize that happiness does not come automatically from success according to our naïve initial imagination and expectation during Phase I. In fact, we might realize that we inflict sufferings upon ourselves in pursuit of that elusive 'success,' and that our struggles for success only add to our pains and stress. We feel that our present mentality and approach have created a large variety of entrapments. We suffer for the lack of a meaningful sense of success, despite our incessant struggles for it, and, even when we have captured all the symbols of success. Thus, we imagine, there should be something wrong with the present definition of success. So now, we like to rediscover the meaning, and means, of 'success,' before it is too late and we get completely old and useless.

We find out in Phase Two that we have been misled to assume we can direct and shape our lives any way we desire. We understand that following the values we have learned and practiced keeps us at the mercy of external forces and other individuals as our sources of satisfaction—but also the main causes of our sufferings. The consequences of our erroneous major life decisions, e.g., a bad career or marriage, are haunting us. We now realize how we have missed our life opportunities due to those wrong decisions. We may find out that our real needs and happiness are not achievable within the crude standards and lifestyles that everybody follows rather blindly. We might at least imagine the possibility of a more meaningful life, question everything we have been doing so far, and perhaps find some motivation to seek other options that could give us freedom, wisdom, 'self'-control, and peace. Whether we act upon our findings and seek a different lifestyle, or at least make some adjustments, is a different matter. However, most often, people do not or cannot make a tangible adjustment.

When we are in our second life phase and ask the question of, 'What is this?', we should remember that, by following the same life routine, the next question awaiting us would be, 'What was it?'; and that in fact would come around very soon. A motivated person may be able to turn his situation around by adjusting his foundation of thoughts, attitude, and actions, once he truly grasps the messages of the forward thinking. He can redeem himself just by pausing his routine life long enough to internalize these awakening messages.

By forward thinking during the second phase of our lives, we want to sensitize our mentality and build up our resilience and wisdom. We also want to reassess our foundation of thoughts and personal life philosophy in hopes of detecting the causes of our failure so far. We hope to find a better philosophy of life in order to avoid getting trapped into the questions of, 'What is this?' and 'What was it?' for the rest of our lives.

But we must also beware of the pitfalls of making drastic changes before establishing our foundation of thoughts and knowing the new criteria for success. So many of us take drastic actions to relieve ourselves from the agony of the question, 'What is this?, when our jobs or marriages do not seem to work. We call it mid-life crisis. However, quitting our jobs or divorcing our spouses and still following the old criteria for finding a new job or spouse would only lead to more frustration and failures. Seeking more pleasure or losing sight of our responsibilities would not solve the problem either, but in fact makes us even more susceptible to the ultimate blow in the third phase.

Phase One Reference

We ask the question 'What my life will be like?' in the first phase of our lives. In the 'forward thinking' domain, this question would take a different meaning and form. If we have established our foundation of thoughts and life based on the awakening messages of forward thinking, asking this question would be redundant in any phase of one's life. In that circumstance, the essentialities of life would not change from one phase to another except that they feel more profound and true. Therefore, looking forward to future outcomes and consequences are meaningless in the way we would normally plan them in the perceived world. In the real world, only our understanding grows while real values remain consistent—cold. The truth does not change; it only becomes clearer and harsher to us with time. Therefore, we learn to become more flexible in our minds and attitude to withstand the sad truth and life's unchangeable rigidity. We do not see success and its criteria in the way we normally do nowadays, and therefore, it cannot be measured now or in the future. In the real world, the only interpretation of success would be 'self'-control, from which true peace and happiness emerge, not sufferings. The test of success is only when we have a decent response for the question of 'What was it?' when we are ready to die.

In all, forward thinking in the first life phase is only for increasing our level of awareness about each circumstance and each thought that would prevail in the future phases of life. If we understand even partially, in Phase One, some of the forward thinking messages, then perhaps we would be mentally prepared to deal with these disappointing facts when they actually hit us. Furthermore, if we could really adjust our thoughts, attitudes, actions, and the criteria of success in the lower phases of life, we increase the possibility of peace, fulfilment, passion, enjoyment, and true happiness in the following life phases.

Forward thinking could trigger a mild state of awakening. We could remain in this domain for a tangible amount of time to attain the real sense of it, rather than passing through it quickly as a tentative awareness. We could reach for a high platform of awareness by absorbing these questions truly and grasping the meanings of those subtle messages. We could reach out for a state of permanent and full awareness, which would lead to deep awakening and the path of wisdom.

A parallel question that emerges during forward thinking is, 'What becomes of my soul (after my earthly life)?' And we already know that perhaps only a few individuals (saints) may have known the answer to this bizarre question, if at all. The question about the future of our souls would remain unanswered forever, as the greatest doubt and mystery of our lives, perhaps even if we were at the summit of the path of wisdom. The existence of a lasting soul, if at all, would surely not be the same type of life experience and feeling as we envision and talk about our spirits now. Most likely, it would be so isolated and different from our earthly life that cannot have any relation to our senses, present existence, naïve contemplations, or be viewed as a continuation of our being. Soul is probably a form of energy teeming around, if that, and then released from, a contained mass we call human existence.

The whole process of life remains full of mysteries, doubts, and decisions. Despite our initial exposure to forward thinking ideas or similar thoughts or experiences, we remain doubtful and cynical about our viable life options. We can neither convince ourselves, nor find the courage, to break away from the norms that so conveniently accommodate our conditioned minds. We do not seem to become really aware of the messages that are in front of us. We simply forget or send them to our unconscious. How many times have we felt our vulnerability and nothingness and soon forgotten them and returned to our expressions and feelings of superiority and Ego domination? How many times have we promised our spirit to change our ways of life when we visited a cemetery, went to the funeral of our young friend, witnessed the miserable life of crippled and helpless people, and saw pictures of masses of children dying in millions from hunger, wars, and neglect? How quickly we lose our compassion and awareness and return to our deep-rooted greed and self-serving thoughts and attitudes!

How soon we forget is no wonder. How our rowdy doubts control the whole domain of our thoughts and render us helpless is no wonder. What is of tremendous wonder is our inability (and unwillingness) to retain a state of self-awareness on a more regular basis! If only we learn to internalize our single and simple awareness experiences, we might eventually find a basic path of wisdom, to make the rest of our lives somewhat easier to go through. What is of tremendous wonder is our inability to let 'forward thinking' rejuvenate our spirits and the foundation of our thoughts!

EPILOGUE

The mysteries of life, love, and happiness are too enigmatic and complex to submit to humans' logic. Besides its vast limitation, in fact, our logic is often too crooked to allow a useful approach for exploring these mysteries. It makes us too dogmatic to ponder new ideas outside the social norms and live with simple notions of contentment. Instead, we insist on extracting happiness from pleasures and sources beyond our control, e.g., through somebody else's attention or submission to us. Even when we face the repercussions of our idiotic thoughts and deeds throughout the human history, we invent weirder ways to fool others and ourselves now in a different way. For example, we seem incapable to find a simple path of life even after we admit that religions have hindered our ability to grasp the meaning of life, love, and happiness. We refuse to see the catastrophes we are causing so recklessly through consumerism and destroying the environment in the process. In fact, we deliberately invent other weird ideas about the purpose of living and our standing in the universe. We convolute even the meaning of spirituality.

Nonetheless, the mere challenge of pondering life's primary mysteries gives us a delightful purpose and it widens our thought processes. Some of us stumble upon some fresh insight and dig deeper in our unconscious for new meanings. We nurture some ideas about love and life to find our special type of happiness—the kind that only each one of us can attain independently by extending sincere emotions and efforts. Fortunately, many of us have the capacity to grasp the bits and pieces of life mysteries.

We also grow some perceptions and adopt tentative answers for love and happiness similar to the ones offered in this book. These occasional discoveries feel like enough rewards for our efforts and a good incentive to stay alive. In return, those occasional feelings help us discover more about ourselves, life, love, and happiness.

We learn that revamping our conditioned mentality, and seeing life in a basic perspective, can curb our dependency on outside sources of love and happiness. Self-awareness enables us find love within ourselves. And we can find happiness in 'self' that is eager to be explored and to help us explore the universe and our spirituality. Then, with all that love and the control of the 'self,' we can most likely make some kind of sense about life, too, at the limited scope of human intelligence and the degree of our contentment.

One thing is certain, however: Just because love and happiness are too illusive and flimsy, and just because life has no particular meaning or purpose, fussing and worrying about nothing make sense. On the other hand, 'living in the now' does not prepare us for the hardships of life, which we must plan for diligently and face positively to bear all the negativities surrounding our lives. We need a solid life philosophy, smart plans, awareness, and stamina to live as smoothly as possible. Then, life, love, and happiness find some meanings, too, once we reach a state of contentment, while we would continue to bask in their blissful mysteries.

www.ingramcontent.com/pod-product-compliance
Lightning Source LLC
Chambersburg PA
CBHW061300110426
42742CB00012BA/1994